THE
SPICE TRAIL

One Hundred Hot Dishes
From India to Indonesia

THE
SPICE TRAIL

One Hundred Hot Dishes
from India to Indonesia

Sandeep Chatterjee

Illustrated by Helen Semmler

TEN SPEED PRESS
Berkeley, California

To Ma and Babai (my parents) who taught me to love and appreciate good food

Text © 1995 Sandeep Chatterjee
Illustrations © 1995 Helen Semmler

TEN SPEED PRESS
P. O. Box 7123
Berkeley, CA 94707

First published in Australasia in 1995 by
Simon & Schuster Australia
20 Barcoo Street, East Roseville NSW 2069

Text designed by Helen Semmler
Typeset in Australia by Asset Typesetting Pty Ltd

Library of Congress Cataloging-in-Publication Data

Chatterjee, Sandeep.
    The spice trail : one hundred hot dishes from India to Indonesia /
    Sandeep Chatterjee.
        p.   cm.
    Includes index.
    ISBN 0-89815-781-1 (pbk.)
    1. Cookery, Oriental. 2. Spices. 3. Condiments. I. Title.
TX724.5.A1C45   1995
641.595 - - dc20   95-12649
                                                              CIP

FIRST PRINTING 1995
Produced by Mandarin Offset
Printed and bound in Hong Kong
1 2 3 4 5 — 99 98 97 96 95

CONTENTS

INTRODUCTION	6
SOUPS	9
FISH AND SEAFOOD	15
POULTRY	43
LAMB	67
PORK	81
BEEF	91
VEGETABLES AND LEGUMES	101
RICE AND NOODLES	113
CURRY PASTES AND POWDERS	129
GLOSSARY	136
INDEX	142
ACKNOWLEDGEMENTS	144

INTRODUCTION

WELCOME TO THE world of Asian cuisine, that exciting mix of spices and *karis* (Tamil for 'sauce'). The use of spices is one of the most creative aspects of Asian cuisine, and the way they are employed can produce widely varying results. Even if recipes are fairly standard throughout a region, the way one household uses spices can be entirely different from that of its neighbours.

To the untrained eye, many *kari* dishes look much the same, but as the recipes in this book show, although dishes may use similar ingredients, such as onion, ginger and garlic, their method of cooking and the choice of additional, often colourful, ingredients make each unique.

Karis originated in India, before travelling abroad into Southeast Asia. On the way they picked up various local ingredients, becoming typical dishes of particular regions. Take, for example, the use of soy sauce in Burma, changing to fish sauce in Thailand, or the addition of fruits and nuts as *karis* travelled westwards. No Anglo-Indian *kari* was complete without its quota of apples or raisins and a side-dish of mango chutney. The abundant use of dried fruits in the *karis* of northwest India is an indication of how adaptable *karis* are.

To follow the evolutionary trail of spices and *karis* is to trace the ancient trading routes from India. Casting off from the Coromandel Coast, Indian traders sailed to Burma, the Malay peninsula and the Straits of Malacca, then Java, Vietnam, Thailand and neighbouring countries. With international trade came the inevitable settling of Indian traders throughout the region, bringing with them their culture and cuisine. The traders were mostly from the Chettinad of south India, which explains the similarity of the cuisines of Southeast Asia to those of south India.

Most of the recipes in this book should be followed more in spirit than in strict adherence to their components and quantities. So, if you don't have one or two of the listed ingredients, you can still proceed with the recipe and achieve a satisfactory result. The way the spices are used also influences texture and flavour: powdered, dry-roasted cumin seeds in yoghurt *raita* enhance the flavour of the dish, but if you substitute unroasted cumin powder, the flavour changes completely. Once you become familiar with the basic methods of cooking a *kari*, the opportunities for experimentation are endless.

As Asians tend to have large, extended families, an Asian meal is never a one-dish affair. On a normal day, a meal would consist of a rice dish plus two or three others. The rice forms the basis of the meal, with the *karis* being served to moisten the rice and facilitate eating.

Textures and colours are very important when coordinating *kari* dishes. You would usually serve a wet dish balanced with a dry vegetable dish and a salad. The salad could contain one vegetable or, at most, a combination of two or three.

Rather than serving an Asian meal course by course, it is customary to lay out all the dishes on a table and let people help themselves. You first place some rice on your plate, then spoon some *kari* on top of it. The rice and the *kari* are then mixed together and eaten. Alcoholic beverages are normally consumed before eating, and drinks are rarely served with the meal.

All the recipes in this book make enough for four people. If catering for more than four, increase the quantities proportionally. However, it would be far better to cook another dish, thereby increasing not only the quantity of the meal but also its variety.

I hope that these recipes will provide a valuable insight into the world of Asian spices and *karis*, and an exciting culinary experience.

SOUPS

IN THE WEST soup is normally one of several courses, and is served at the start of a meal. This is not so in Asia, where soup is usually consumed as a one-dish filler between meals or as a side dish to the meal proper. It tends, too, to be a clear broth or stock, flavoured with herbs and spices, meat, fish or poultry.

The following recipes are among the most popular in Southeast Asia. In most cases the stock used is very light, allowing the flavours of the herbs and spices to infuse into the liquid.

OMELETTE SOUP WITH PORK AND CORIANDER (CILANTRO)

Moo Kai Nam — Thailand

250 g (½ lb) lean pork, thinly
    sliced
a little salt
4 cups (1 L, 1¾ imp. pints)
    water
a few coriander (cilantro) roots
    or sprigs
3 tablespoons vegetable oil
1 tablespoon chopped garlic
2 medium onions, chopped
1 tablespoon chopped galangal
1–1½ cups (125–185 g, 4–6 oz)
    shredded cabbage
2 tablespoons fish sauce
1 tablespoon ground white
    pepper
salt, to taste
4 eggs, beaten
a little vegetable oil
a few extra coriander (cilantro)
    sprigs, to garnish
4 young spring onions
    (scallions), green part only,
    sliced

A VERY PLEASANT and light soup commonly sold on roadside stalls. Though originally of Thai origin, it is now found in different versions throughout Southeast Asia. Substituting other meats for the pork works very well in this dish. The coriander sprigs added just before serving not only give this soup an attactive appearance, but also impart a fresh, distinctive flavour.

Method: Rub the pork all over with salt. Place in a medium pan with the water and bring to the boil. Add the coriander roots or sprigs. Simmer for 10–12 minutes until cooked. Remove from the heat and set aside.

Heat the oil in a medium pan. Add the garlic and sauté until golden brown. Add the onion and sauté for 2–3 minutes, until soft. Now add the galangal and cabbage. Stir-fry for 2–3 minutes before adding the pork and its cooking liquid. Simmer over a medium heat for 5–7 minutes. Add the fish sauce and pepper. Check the seasoning and adjust with salt if necessary.

Meanwhile, add the eggs to a wok coated with a little oil. Cook into an omelette, then remove from the wok and allow to cool. Roll up the cooled omelette and cut into strips.

Ladle the soup into serving bowls. Garnish each serving with some omelette, coriander sprigs and spring onion. Serve immediately.

RICE SOUP WITH PRAWNS (SHRIMP)
Kao Tom — Thailand

2 tablespoons vegetable oil
2 stalks celery, sliced
4 cups (1 L, 1¾ imp. pints)
water
1½ cups (125 g, 4 oz) cooked
rice
2 tablespoons fish sauce
1 tablespoon ground white
pepper
6 cloves garlic, peeled and
sliced
375 g (¾ lb) small prawns
(shrimp), peeled and
deveined
8 thin slices fresh ginger
2 spring onions (scallions),
green part only, chopped
a few coriander (cilantro)
sprigs, to garnish

A SIMPLE YET very refreshing soup. Unlike in Western cooking, most of the soups found throughout Southeast Asia are cooked with water instead of stock. As a result, they are very light and always take on the flavour of the added herbs. The addition of coriander or ginger just before serving gives this soup one of the many beautiful aromas associated with Southeast Asian cuisine.

Method: Heat 1 tablespoon of the oil in a medium pan. Add the celery and sauté for 3–5 minutes. Add the water and bring to a fast boil. Reduce the heat and simmer for 1 minute before adding the rice, fish sauce and white pepper. Continue to simmer gently.

Meanwhile, heat the remaining oil in a medium pan. Add the garlic and cook over a medium heat until golden brown. Add the prawns and stir-fry for 3–5 minutes. Add to the soup and simmer for 1–2 minutes.

Ladle the soup into serving bowls. Add two slices of ginger to each serving and garnish with the spring onion and coriander sprigs.
Serve immediately.

SPICY CHICKEN SOUP WITH PRAWNS (SHRIMP)

Soto Ayam — Singapore

8 medium prawns (shrimp)
4 cups (1 L, 1¾ imp. pints)
    water
2 tablespoons vegetable oil
2 medium onions, chopped
2 tablespoons chopped ginger
1 tablespoon chopped garlic
2 teaspoons ground turmeric
1 tablespoon red chilli powder
250 g (½ lb) chicken thigh
    meat, skinned and cut into
    1 cm (½ in.) dice
8 candlenuts (cashew nuts or
    pine nuts can be used if
    candlenuts are unavailable)
2 teaspoons cracked black
    peppercorns
1 tablespoon soy sauce
1 tablespoon chopped coriander
    (cilantro) leaves, to garnish

A POPULAR CHICKEN soup usually sold on the many food stalls around Singapore in one form or another. It is quite a refreshing dish, especially on cold, rainy days. When served with fresh, crusty bread, it makes a perfect meal.

Method: Peel and devein the prawns. Do not discard the shells. Set the prawns aside. Combine the water and prawn shells in a saucepan. Bring to the boil, then reduce the heat and simmer for 3–5 minutes. Strain the prawn stock and reserve. Discard the shells.

Heat the oil in a medium pan over a medium heat. Add the onion and sauté until transparent. Add the ginger, garlic, turmeric and chilli powder. Stir-fry for 1–2 minutes. Add the diced chicken and stir-fry for a further 1–2 minutes. Add the reserved prawn stock and bring to a boil. Reduce to a simmer and cook, uncovered, until the chicken is nearly done, 10–12 minutes. Reduce to a low simmer.

Meanwhile, combine the candlenuts and peppercorns. Grind to a powder in a spice or coffee grinder. Mix this powder with the soy sauce to make a smooth paste (add a little water, if necessary, to blend). Stir into the simmering soup. Add the prawns and cook until done, 3–4 minutes. Serve hot, garnished with the coriander.

SEAFOOD AND LEMON GRASS SOUP
Tom Yum Tah Leh — Thailand

3¾ cups (935 mL, 1½ imp.
   pints) water
1 stalk lemon grass
1 tablespoon galangal
a few fresh Kaffir lime leaves
1 tablespoon chopped ginger
⅔ cup (150 mL, 5 fl oz) coconut
   milk
2 tablespoons fish sauce
250 g (½ lb) white fish fillet,
   cut into 2 cm (1 in.) pieces
125 g (¼ lb) small prawns
   (shrimp), peeled and
   deveined
2 tablespoons coriander
   (cilantro) leaves
3 small spring onions
   (scallions), green part only,
   sliced

THE COMBINATION OF SEAFOOD and lemon grass makes this a very refreshing soup. You can easily turn it into a main course by adding some cooked rice or rice vermicelli.

Method: Bring the water to a boil in a deep saucepan. Add the lemon grass, galangal, Kaffir lime leaves, ginger, coconut milk and fish sauce. Simmer for about 10 minutes. Add the fish pieces and simmer for a further 2 minutes. Add the prawns and cook for 3–4 minutes, until done. Stir in the coriander.

   Ladle the soup into serving bowls. Garnish each serving with some spring onion and serve immediately.

FISH AND SEAFOOD

THE COUNTRIES OF ASIA have extensive coastlines and some of the most fertile seas in the world. It is no wonder, then, that cuisine in the region relies so heavily on the use of seafood. Fish is pickled, dried, preserved and salted, and is used in numerous permutations and combinations. In coastal India, an otherwise strictly vegetarian society, where the mere name of animal flesh is offensive, fish is eaten readily and is looked upon as a fruit from the ocean. In areas where coconut palms grow in abundance, dishes are usually coconut based. Elsewhere, tomatoes or onions may replace the coconut.

Although I have used local Asian fish in these recipes, almost any other fish can be substituted, so long as it is fresh and firm-fleshed. If you buy frozen fish, do so in small quantities, as fish stored over long periods start losing flavour. Pre-cooked shellfish are good for cold dishes, but for curries I always prefer to cook them with the meal. Medium-size prawns or shrimp are usually the tastiest and are best cooked in their shells.

GRILLED SNAPPER WITH GREEN MANGO CHUTNEY

Machi Chutney — Malabar Coast

4 plate-size snapper or any
    other flat fish (375 g, ¾ lb),
    cleaned and scaled
2 tablespoons ground turmeric
3 tablespoons red chilli powder
salt, to taste
a little vegetable oil

GREEN MANGO CHUTNEY
1 cup (250 mL, 8 fl oz) plain
    yoghurt
2 tablespoons chopped green
    (unripe) mango
2 tablespoons chopped spring
    onions (scallion)
1 tablespoon chopped ginger
4 green chilli peppers, chopped
2 teaspoons chopped garlic
1 tablespoon palm sugar or
    brown sugar
salt, to taste

THE COOL YOGHURT and green mango blend to give
the chutney used with this dish its unique flavour.
Any flat fish is ideal for this recipe. If you wish, you
can use fillets instead of whole fish. If you do, dust
the fillets in a little plain (all-purpose) flour before
grilling or pan-frying.

Method: Make gashes on each side of the fish. Rub
with the turmeric, chilli powder and salt. Set aside
for 10–15 minutes.

Meanwhile, whisk the yoghurt in a bowl. Stir in
the mango, spring onions, ginger, chilli peppers,
garlic and palm sugar. Add salt and set the chutney
aside until ready to serve.

Lightly baste the fish with a little oil. Cook on
both sides under a medium-hot grill (broiler). Be
careful not to overcook as this will make the fish dry.
(Alternatively, shallow-fry the fish in a frying pan or
skillet.) Quickly drain the fish on paper towels or
absorbent kitchen paper. Serve hot, accompanied by
the Green Mango Chutney.

SHALLOW-FRIED FISH MEKONG
Ca Mekong — Vietnam

4 plate-size fish (375 g, ¾ lb),
    cleaned and scaled
salt, to taste
rice flour, for dusting
5 tablespoons oil
4 fresh red chilli peppers, cut
    into julienne
3 spring onions (scallions),
    roughly chopped
1 tablespoon ginger, cut into
    julienne
2 teaspoons tamarind pulp
2 tablespoons fish sauce
1 tablespoon brown or
    palm sugar

THIS IS A VERY popular way to serve whole fish. Usually the fish is deep-fried, but I prefer to shallow fry as I feel it is both easier and more healthy. You can use any whole fish that you fancy for this recipe.

Method: Cut gashes on both sides of the fish. Rub a little salt over the surface of the fish, then dust with rice flour.

Heat 3 tablespoons of the oil in a frying pan or skillet. Add the fish and cook on both sides. Place the fish on a serving dish and set aside to keep warm.

Heat the remaining oil in a clean pan. Add the chilli peppers, spring onions and ginger. Stir-fry for 1–2 minutes, then add the tamarind pulp, fish sauce and sugar. Mix thoroughly. Pour the sauce over the fish. Serve immediately.

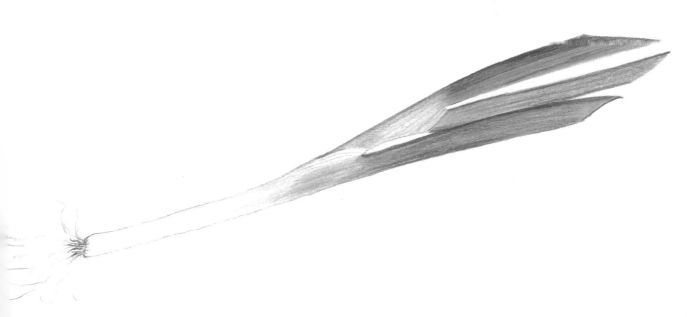

MARINATED FISH IN CURRY SAUCE
Nga Hin — Burma

500 g (1 lb) fish fillets
1 tablespoon ground turmeric
1 tablespoon fish sauce
4 tablespoons sesame oil
2 medium onions, chopped
2 tablespoons chopped ginger
1 tablespoon chopped garlic
1 stalk lemon grass
1 cm (¹/₂ in.) piece of blachan,
    dry-roasted (see glossary)
2 large tomatoes, chopped
4 green chilli peppers, chopped
1 tablespoon fish sauce (extra)
2 tablespoons chopped
    coriander (cilantro) leaves

FISH AND RICE form the staple diet of Burma. Fish in some form is always served either as a main or side dish. Here is a recipe in which the flavours blend to make a unique dish.

Method: Marinate the fish in the turmeric and fish sauce while preparing the other ingredients.

Heat the sesame oil in a medium pan. Add the onion and sauté over a medium heat for 5–7 minutes, until soft. Add the ginger, garlic, lemon grass and blachan. Sauté for 2–3 minutes. Add the tomatoes, chilli peppers and extra fish sauce. Simmer for 5–7 minutes. Now add the fish and cook for 5–7 minutes, until done. Serve hot, garnished with the coriander.

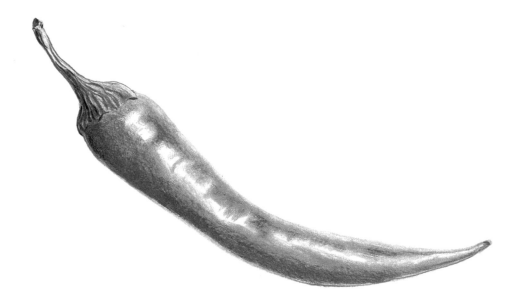

FISH CALDINE

Meen Caldine — Goa

4 fish steaks (such as kingfish
   or jewfish), about 125 g
   (¼ lb) each
salt, to taste
2 tablespoons coriander seeds
2 teaspoons cumin seeds
2 teaspoons whole black
   peppercorns
2 tablespoons poppy seeds
2 whole cloves
2½ cm (1 in.) stick of
   cinnamon
2 green cardamom pods
a little water
2 tablespoons vegetable oil
2 medium onions, chopped
2 teaspoons ground turmeric
4 green chilli peppers, slit
   lengthways
2 cups (500 mL, 16 fl oz)
   coconut milk
2 medium tomatoes, quartered

THIS DISH ORIGINATES in Goa, the former Portuguese territory on the west coast of India. Goa is famous for its golden beaches, its relaxed lifestyle and its inhabitants' addiction to good food and wine. Goanese cuisine is typified by its use of coconut and is very similar to the cuisines of south India and Thailand. This particular recipe is a very popular festive dish.

Method: Rub the fish steaks with salt and set aside.

Meanwhile, dry-roast the coriander and cumin seeds, peppercorns, poppy seeds, cloves, cinnamon and cardamom together over a moderate heat, until fragrant. Cool for a minute or two, then grind to a powder in a spice or coffee grinder. Place the powder in a bowl and add just enough water to make a thick paste. Set aside.

Heat the oil in a medium frying pan or skillet. Add the onion and sauté until soft. Add the paste and the turmeric. Sauté over a moderate heat for 2–3 minutes, until the paste is fragrant. Add the chilli peppers and coconut milk. Bring to a fast boil, stirring constantly, then reduce the heat to a simmer. Simmer for 5 minutes before adding the fish steaks. Cook for a further 8–10 minutes, until done.

Just before removing from the heat, add the tomatoes and stir through gently. Check the seasoning and add salt if necessary. Serve hot with boiled rice.

WHOLE SNAPPER WITH PEPPERS

Meen Recheade — Goa

4 plate-size snapper (about 375 g, ³/₄ lb), cleaned and scaled
salt, to taste
6 dried red chilli peppers, seeded
¹/₄ cup (60 mL, 2 fl oz) white vinegar
1 tablespoon cumin seeds
1 tablespoon chopped garlic
1 tablespoon ground turmeric
1 tablespoon white peppercorns
1 tablespoon chopped ginger
4 green (small) cardamom pods
2¹/₂ cm (1 in.) stick of cinnamon
3 whole cloves
1 tablespoon granulated sugar
1 tablespoon dried prawns (shrimp)
2 tablespoons tamarind water (see glossary)
rice flour, for dusting
vegetable oil, for shallow-frying

ANOTHER GOANESE FAVOURITE, this dish works best with whole fish, but any firm-fleshed fish fillets can be used. If you use fillets, spread the paste on both sides. The red chilli peppers give the fish a unique, deep red colour. If you do not want a fiery hot dish, however, replace the chilli peppers with paprika.

Method: Slit the flesh along both sides of the spine of the fish. With a sharp knife, ease the flesh off the bones. Remove the bones, leaving the fish intact. (You can ask your fishmonger to do this for you.) Rub the fish lightly with salt and set aside.

Soak the chilli peppers in the vinegar and let stand for 3–5 minutes. Combine the cumin seeds, garlic, turmeric, peppercorns, ginger, cardamom, cinnamon, cloves, sugar and dried prawns in an electric blender or food processor. Add the tamarind water and the soaked chilli peppers and vinegar. Blend or process to a fine paste.

Rub the inside of the fish with this paste, then dust the outside with rice flour. Shallow-fry in the vegetable oil in a frying pan or skillet for 5–6 minutes each side, until cooked. Serve with a green salad and crusty bread.

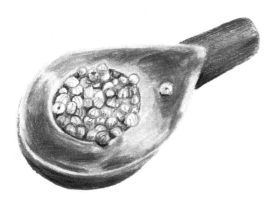

FISH WITH FENUGREEK LEAVES
Machi Methi — India

4 fish steaks, about 375 g
   (³/₄ lb) each
salt, to taste
4 tablespoons vegetable oil
2 medium onions, sliced
2 tablespoons chopped ginger
1 tablespoon chopped garlic
1 tablespoon red chilli powder
2 teaspoons ground turmeric
2 medium tomatoes, chopped
1¼ cups (300 g, 10 oz) plain
   yoghurt
4 tablespoons chopped
   fenugreek leaves (if using
   dried fenugreek leaves, use
   only 2 tablespoons)
2 tablespoons chopped
   coriander (cilantro) leaves

THIS DISH COMES from Bombay, the most cosmopolitan city in India. People from all parts of the country have made Bombay their home, bringing with them their cultures, cuisines and religions. The local cuisine is really a fusion of different regional cooking styles. The inspiration for the fenugreek leaves (*machi methi*) comes from Bengal and the Punjab — two very diverse regions of India. Though the best results are obtained by using fresh leaves, these are not readily available. Dried leaves can be substituted, and are available from Asian food stores.

Method: Place the fish steaks in a bowl and rub all over with salt. Set aside.

   Heat the oil in a wide, shallow pan. Add the onion and sauté over a high heat until golden brown. Reduce the heat and add the ginger and garlic. Sauté for 1–2 minutes. Add the chilli powder and turmeric. Sauté for a further 1–2 minutes. Now add the tomatoes, increase the heat and cook for 4–5 minutes.

   Meanwhile, whisk the yoghurt until smooth and set aside. Add the fenugreek leaves to the pan and stir-fry for a few minutes. Add the yoghurt and bring to a fast boil, stirring continuously so that the yoghurt does not curdle. Reduce the heat and simmer for 4–5 minutes. Add the fish steaks and cook for 8–10 minutes, until done. Check the seasoning and adjust with salt if necessary. Stir in the coriander. Serve hot.

FISH WITH TOMATOES AND TAMARIND
Pla Gaeng Phed — Thailand

2 tablespoons vegetable oil
2 medium onions, chopped
2 medium tomatoes, chopped
2 tablespoons sambal ulek
1 tablespoon shrimp paste
1 tablespoon raw sugar
2 tablespoons tamarind water
(see glossary)
1 mackerel, cleaned and scaled,
cut into steaks, or about
500 g (1 lb) other small fish,
cleaned and scaled, but left
whole
salt, to taste

THIS IS A DISH from the Chiang Rai region of Thailand. Because of Thailand's proximity to Burma, its cuisine is more Burmese than Thai. The blending of tomatoes and tamarind is typical of the curries of south India, and also forms an integral part of Burmese cuisine.

Method: Heat the oil in a medium pan. Add the onions and sauté until soft. Add the tomatoes and cook over a medium heat until the sauce becomes soft and pulpy. Now add the sambal ulek, shrimp paste, sugar and tamarind water. Simmer for 3–5 minutes. Add the fish and continue to cook over a medium heat for 5–8 minutes, until done. Check the seasoning and adjust with salt if necessary. Serve hot with boiled rice.

PAN-FRIED FISH WITH SOY SAUCE

Nga Gyaw — Burma

4 firm-fleshed fish fillets,
  about 250 g (¹/₂ lb) each
2 teaspoons ground turmeric
a little salt
4 tablespoons sesame oil
4 tablespoons soy sauce
scant ¹/₃ cup (100 mL, 3 fl oz)
  water
2 tablespoons chopped ginger
2 tablespoons spring onions
  (scallions), finely chopped
a few coriander (cilantro)
  sprigs, to garnish

A VERY SIMPLE DISH, this recipe works very well with fresh fish fillets, as the soy sauce and ginger combine to bring out the best in the fish. It can also be made successfully using whole fish.

Method: Rub the fish fillets with the turmeric and just a little salt. Set aside for a few minutes.

Heat the oil in a large frying pan or skillet. When hot, add the fish and cook on both sides for 2–3 minutes, until done. Lay out on a serving platter and set aside to keep warm in a warming tray or cooling oven.

Add the soy sauce and water to the pan the fish was cooked in. Bring to the boil and simmer for 2–4 minutes, until the liquid has reduced in volume by half. Stir in the ginger and spring onions. Turn off the heat and let the sauce stand for 1 minute. Serve garnished with the coriander sprigs.

The sauce can be served separately or poured over the fish fillets.

PARSEE FISH WITH MINT CHUTNEY
Patrani Machi — India

MINT CHUTNEY
*2¹⁄₃ cups (225 g, 7 oz) desiccated
    (shredded) coconut*
*scant 1 cup (225 mL, 7 fl oz)
    coconut cream*
2 teaspoons ground turmeric
*2 tablespoons mango chutney
    (use a ready-made chutney
    available from good
    supermarkets or Asian
    food stores)*
1 teaspoon cumin seeds
1 bunch of mint leaves
1 bunch of coriander (cilantro)
sugar, to taste
1 tablespoon white vinegar
*2¹⁄₂ cm (1 in.) piece of fresh
    ginger*
3 cloves garlic

PARSEE FISH
*4 banana leaves, to wrap the
    fish*
*4 small perch fillets, about
    250 g (¹⁄₂ lb) each*
salt, to taste
1 teaspoon ground turmeric
*2 teaspoons small red chilli
    peppers, chopped*
juice of 1 lemon

A WEIGHT WATCHER'S delight from the west coast of
India — steamed fish in banana leaves.

Mint chutney: Place all the ingredients for the
chutney in an electric blender or food processor.
Blend or process until well combined. Remove to
a clean bowl and place in the refrigerator to chill.

Parsee fish: Cut the banana leaves into rectangles
large enough to wrap the fish. Heat the leaves over a
flame or hotplate to soften them — this makes them
easier to fold.
   Sprinkle the fish with the salt, turmeric, chilli
peppers and lemon juice. Lay each piece of fish flat
on a banana leaf. Top with about 2 tablespoons of the
Mint Chutney. Spread the chutney evenly over the
top, then fold the banana leaf around the fish.
Leave in the refrigerator all day, or in the freezer
for 10–15 minutes to set the chutney.
   Steam the fish in a steamer for about
8–10 minutes. Serve hot.

SWEET AND SOUR FISH

Ambotik — Goa

10 whole red chilli peppers
2 teaspoons cumin seeds
2 teaspoons black peppercorns
2 teaspoons coriander seeds
1 tablespoon chopped garlic
1 tablespoon chopped ginger
2 teaspoons ground turmeric
a little water
500 g (1 lb) firm-fleshed white
    fish fillets
salt, to taste (for the sauce)
4 tablespoons vegetable oil
2 medium onions, chopped
2/3 cup (150 mL, 5 fl oz) water
2 tablespoons tamarind water
    (see glossary)
2 teaspoons brown sugar

A SIMPLE FISH dish from Goa, usually eaten with plain boiled rice. This a country style of cooking in which a few commonly available spices are blended with plain water and tamarind to give the dish its earthy flavour. *Ambotik* uses catfish, which is freely available in and around Goa's lagoons.

Method: Dry-roast the chilli peppers, cumin, peppercorns and coriander over a medium heat until fragrant. Grind to a fine powder in a spice or coffee grinder. Place in an electric blender or food processor with the garlic, ginger and turmeric. Blend or process into a wet paste, adding as little water as possible to do so.
   Cut the fish into small pieces and rub with salt. Set aside.
   Heat the oil in a pan. Add the onion and sauté until soft. Add the wet paste and stir-fry over a medium heat for 3–5 minutes. Add the water, tamarind water and sugar. Bring to a fast boil, then let simmer for 4–5 minutes. Add the fish pieces and simmer over a medium heat for 5–6 minutes, until cooked. Check the seasoning and adjust the flavour by adding a little more sugar or tamarind if required. Remove from the heat and serve hot with boiled rice.

MARINATED FISH WITH MUSTARD

Sorse Mach — Bangladesh

1 tablespoon mustard seeds
3 medium tomatoes, chopped
4 whole red chilli peppers
1½ cups (375 mL, 12 fl oz)
    water
4 fish steaks, about 125 g
    (¼ lb) each
1½ tablespoons ground
    turmeric
1 tablespoon red chilli powder
salt, to taste
4 tablespoons mustard or
    vegetable oil
2 teaspoons panch phora
    (see glossary)
salt, to taste
2 tablespoons coriander
    (cilantro) leaves, chopped

A VARIETY OF CARP is normally used for this festive dish from Bangladesh, but any firm-fleshed fish can be substituted. The quantity of mustard in this recipe is very important as even just a little too much will make the dish bitter. Mustard oil is the traditional cooking medium, but vegetable oil can be substituted if desired.

Method: Mix the mustard seeds, tomatoes and chilli peppers with 1 cup (250 mL, 8 fl oz) of water and process in a blender till smooth.

Marinate the fish in 2 teaspoons of turmeric, the chilli powder and salt. Set aside.

Heat the oil in a large pan. When smoking, remove and cool to medium hot. Mix the remaining turmeric and water and set aside. Add the *panch phora* to the oil. When it starts to change colour, add the turmeric water. Reduce over a medium heat until almost all the water has evaporated. Now add the blended paste. Bring to a fast boil, reduce the heat and simmer for 5–8 minutes. Add the salt if needed. Add the fish and cook for 6–8 minutes, until done, depending upon the thickness of the steak. Garnish with the coriander and serve immediately.

WHOLE FISH IN RED SAUCE
Ikan Bakkar — Indonesia

4 plate-size snapper (about
   375 g, ³/₄ lb), cleaned and
   scaled
salt, to taste
2 tablespoons white vinegar
6 tablespoons vegetable oil
2 medium onions, chopped
1 tablespoon sambal ulek
1 cm (¹/₂ in.) piece of blachan,
   dry-roasted (see glossary)
2 medium tomatoes, chopped
freshly ground black pepper,
   to taste
2 tablespoons coriander
   (cilantro) leaves, chopped

THIS DISH WORKS well with any whole fish, such as snapper, trout or mackerel, or even fish fillets. However, the fish should be absolutely fresh.

Method: Make 4 evenly spaced gashes on either side of the snapper. Rub the whole fish with the salt and vinegar. Set aside for 10–12 minutes. Heat 4 tablespoons of the oil in a pan. Shallow-fry the fish on both sides for 5–7 minutes, until cooked. Alternatively, you can grill the fish.

   Heat the remaining 2 tablespoons of oil in a medium pan and add the onion. Cook until soft. Add the sambal ulek and blachan. Stir-fry for 1 minute. Add the tomatoes and black pepper. Cook over a medium heat until the sauce is thick and pulpy. Stir in half the coriander. Spoon the sauce over the fish and serve hot, sprinkled with the remaining coriander.

PRAWN (SHRIMP) CURRY WITH THAI EGGPLANT

Gaeng Gung Puang — Thailand

2 tablespoons vegetable oil
2 tablespoons green curry paste
(see page 130)
½ cup (60 g, 2 oz) Thai
eggplant or fresh green peas
a few holy basil leaves
6 Kaffir lime leaves, torn
4 green chilli peppers
2 stalks lemon grass, sliced
2 cups (500 mL, 16 fl oz)
coconut milk
1 tablespoon fish sauce
2 teaspoons brown sugar
20–25 (875 g, 1¾ lb) medium
prawns (shrimp), peeled and
deveined
2 tablespoons coriander
(cilantro) leaves, chopped

SMALL THAI EGGPLANTS grow in clusters and are very pretty to look at. They have a bitter taste which gives the curry an added, unusual tang. You can substitute green peas if Thai eggplants are not available.

Method: Heat the oil in a large pan, add the curry paste and cook over a medium heat for a few minutes. Add the Thai eggplant, basil leaves, Kaffir lime leaves, chilli peppers and lemon grass. Stir-fry for 3–5 minutes. Now add the coconut milk, fish sauce and sugar. Bring the sauce to the boil, then simmer it for 5–7 minutes. Add the prawns and cook for 4–7 minutes, until done. Add the coriander to the dish and serve hot with boiled rice.

CEYLON PRAWN (SHRIMP) CURRY

Isso Kari — Sri Lanku

salt, to taste
2 teaspoons ground turmeric
2 tablespoons red chilli powder
625 g (1¼ lb) prawns (shrimp),
    peeled and deveined
4 tablespoons vegetable oil
1 teaspoon fenugreek seeds
a few curry leaves
2 medium onions, finely
    chopped
2 tablespoons chopped ginger
1 tablespoon chopped garlic
2 tablespoons Ceylon curry
    powder (see page 133)
1½ cups (375 mL, 12 fl oz)
    coconut milk
1 tablespoon tamarind pulp

PRAWNS ARE ALWAYS very popular. For curries I prefer the medium or small prawns, rather than the large varieties, because they are more tender and have a sweeter taste.

Method: Combine the salt, turmeric and 2 teaspoons of chilli powder. Coat the prawns with this mixture and set aside.

Heat the oil in a large pan. Fry the prawns quickly without cooking them through. Remove and set aside. To the same pan, add the fenugreek, curry leaves and onion. Stir-fry until the onion is soft. Add the ginger and garlic, and stir-fry for 1–2 minutes. Now add the remaining chilli powder and the curry powder. Stir-fry for a further 1–2 minutes. Add the coconut milk and season with salt if necessary. Bring to a boil, then reduce the heat and simmer for 5–8 minutes. Add the tamarind pulp, mixing thoroughly. Add the prawns and simmer for 4–5 minutes, until pink. Serve with boiled rice.

BATTERED PRAWNS (SHRIMP) IN CURRY SAUCE

Bung Khongh — Cambodia

20 (875 g, 1¾ lb) medium
  prawns (shrimp), peeled and
  deveined
1 tablespoon soy sauce
2 teaspoons ground turmeric
2 teaspoons red chilli powder
1 tablespoon cumin seeds
1 tablespoon coriander seeds
2 teaspoons fennel seeds
2 medium onions, chopped
2 tablespoons chopped ginger
1 tablespoon chopped garlic
6 green chilli peppers
a little water
vegetable oil, for deep-frying
3 tablespoons vegetable oil
⅓ cup (90 mL, 3 fl oz) water
1 tablespoon tamarind pulp
1 tablespoon fish sauce

BATTER
¼ cup (30 g, 1 oz) rice flour
½ cup (125 g, 4 oz) plain
  (all-purpose) flour
¼ cup (30 g, 1 oz) cornflour
  (cornstarch)
about ¾ cup (185 mL, 6 fl oz)
  water
2 egg whites

THIS IS AN INTRIGUING and unusual recipe.
The prawns are dipped in batter, then fried.
The curry is made separately and the prawns added
to it. This method of cooking is very common in
China, but is not normally used in India.

Method: Marinate the prawns in the soy sauce,
turmeric and chilli powder while preparing the
remaining ingredients.

Meanwhile, dry-roast the cumin, coriander and
fennel seeds. Grind into a powder and set aside.
Put the onion, ginger, garlic and green chilli peppers
in an electric blender or food processor. Blend to a
paste, using a little water to facilitate blending.
Set aside.

To make the batter, combine the rice flour, plain
flour and cornflour in a bowl. Gradually add the
water, whisking as you do so. Use just enough water
to achieve a smooth consistency. Whisk the egg
whites until stiff. Lightly fold through the batter.
Dip the prawns into the batter. Deep-fry in vegetable
oil until golden in colour. Set aside.

Heat the 3 tablespoons of oil in a pan. Add the
paste of onion, chillies, ginger and garlic and sauté
for 4–5 minutes. Now add the dry powder and sauté
for a further 1–2 minutes. Add the water and simmer
for about 5 minutes. Add the tamarind pulp and fish
sauce. Simmer for 1–2 minutes. Just before serving,
add the battered prawns. Serve hot.

SPICY PRAWNS (SHRIMP) IN COCONUT MILK
Narial Jhinga — Maldives

2 tablespoons chopped ginger
1 tablespoon chopped garlic
1 tablespoon ground turmeric
2 tablespoons red chilli powder
2 tablespoons white vinegar
4 tablespoons sesame oil
2 medium onions, chopped
2 medium tomatoes, chopped
salt, to taste
¾ cup (185 mL, 6 fl oz) coconut
   milk
500 g (1 lb) prawns (shrimp),
   peeled and deveined
1 tablespoon cracked black
   peppercorns
2 tablespoons coriander
   (cilantro) leaves, chopped
extra coriander (cilantro)
   leaves, to garnish

WITH ITS USE OF VINEGAR and coconut milk, this spicy prawn dish from the Muslim Maldives combines the cuisines of west and south Asia to create food with a unique flavour.

Method: Mix the ginger, garlic, turmeric and chilli powder with the vinegar to make a paste.

Heat the sesame oil in a large pan and add the onion. Sauté until the onion is soft. Add the paste to the pan and stir for 3–4 minutes over a gentle heat.

Add the tomatoes and salt. Increase the heat to medium and cook until the tomatoes soften, then add the coconut milk. Reduce the heat and simmer for about 5 minutes. Now add the prawns and cook for 4–5 minutes, until done. Add the peppercorns and coriander.

Serve topped with the extra coriander leaves.

Everyday Prawn (Shrimp) Curry

Soongtha Kari — Goa

6 dried red chilli peppers
1 tablespoon cumin seeds
2 tablespoons coriander seeds
2½ cm (1 in.) piece of
   cinnamon stick
2 whole cloves
2 whole cardamom pods
a little water
2 tablespoons vegetable oil
2 medium onions, sliced
1 tablespoon chopped ginger
1 tablespoon chopped garlic
1 tablespoon ground turmeric
2 cups (500 mL, 16 fl oz)
   coconut milk
4 green chilli peppers, slit
   lengthways
2 tablespoons tamarind water
   (see glossary)
2 medium tomatoes, quartered
500 g (1 lb) prawns (shrimp),
   peeled and deveined
salt, to taste

A COMMONLY FOUND curry from the west coast of India, which can be also be made with fish or vegetables. Often, a combination of main ingredients is used. This is a very simple curry, based on coconut and red chillies, and flavoured with ginger and garlic.

Method: Dry-roast the red chilli peppers, cumin, coriander, cinnamon, cloves and cardamom. Grind to a fine powder in a spice or coffee grinder. Place in a bowl and add just enough water to make a paste. Set aside.

Heat the vegetable oil in a large pan. Add the onion and sauté until soft. Add the ginger and garlic. Sauté for 1 minute. Now add the paste and turmeric. Sauté for a few minutes. Add the coconut milk and green chilli peppers. Bring to a fast boil, reduce the heat and simmer for about 5 minutes.

Add the tamarind water and tomatoes and simmer for 5–7 minutes. Add the prawns and simmer for 4–7 minutes, until cooked. Check the seasoning and add salt if necessary. Remove from the heat and serve hot.

MARINATED FRIED PRAWNS (SHRIMP)

Singapore

500 g (1 lb) green prawns
(shrimp), peeled and
deveined
2 teaspoons five-spice powder
2 tablespoons soy sauce
juice of ½ lemon
1 tablespoon finely chopped
ginger
vegetable oil, for deep-frying

BATTER
1 large egg
½– ⅔ cup (125–150 mL,
4–5 fl oz) water
1 cup (125 g, 4 oz) rice flour
2 tablespoons red chilli powder
1 tablespoon ground turmeric
2 tablespoons ground coriander
salt, to taste

THIS IS ANOTHER typically Singaporean dish. The prawn marinade combines Indian and Chinese influences, and frying the food in a rice flour batter is very south Indian.

Method: Place the prawns in a bowl. Add the five-spice powder, soy sauce, lemon juice and ginger. Mix well and leave to marinate for 15–20 minutes.

Meanwhile, beat the egg with ½ cup (125 mL, 4 fl oz) of water. Set aside. Combine the rice flour, chilli powder, turmeric, coriander and salt in a bowl. Add a little water and mix into a thick paste (add more water if necessary). Pour in the egg and water mixture, whisking continuously. Add extra water if the batter is too thick (it should be the consistency of flapjack batter). Allow to rest for 10–15 minutes.

Heat the oil in a deep-fryer or heavy saucepan over a medium heat. Dip the prawns in the batter and deep-fry in the oil until golden in colour. Drain on paper towels (absorbent kitchen paper). Serve with a spicy dip.

PINEAPPLE SHRIMP CURRY

Gaeng Kung — Thailand

3 tablespoons vegetable oil
3 tablespoons red curry paste
   (see page 131)
2 tablespoons tamarind water
   (see glossary)
1 tablespoon palm or brown
   sugar
2 tablespoons fish sauce
2 cups (500 mL, 16 fl oz)
   coconut milk
4–5 Kaffir lime leaves, torn
salt, to taste
500 g (1 lb) prawns (shrimp),
   peeled and deveined
¼ small pineapple (about
   1 g, (4 oz)), peeled and finely
   chopped
1 red chilli pepper, split
   (optional)

THIS DELICATELY SWEET and sour curry originates from the central plains of Thailand. Pineapple, prawns and tamarind combine to give the dish a flavour unlike any other.

Method: Heat the oil in a large pan over a medium heat. Add the curry paste and sauté for 3–4 minutes. Add the tamarind water, palm or brown sugar, fish sauce, coconut milk and Kaffir lime leaves. Bring to the boil, then reduce the heat and simmer for 5 minutes. Check the seasoning and add salt if necessary. Add the prawns and simmer for 3–5 minutes, until cooked.

Serve hot with boiled rice, garnished with the pineapple pieces and red chilli pepper (if using).

SHRIMP IN COCONUT AND FENNEL

Chemmen Serringam — Singapore

3 tablespoons vegetable oil
1 teaspoon mustard seeds
2 teaspoons fennel seeds
a few curry leaves
2 medium onions, chopped
1 tablespoon chopped ginger
1 teaspoon ground turmeric
2 teaspoons red chilli powder
2 medium tomatoes, chopped
4 tablespoons desiccated
   (shredded) coconut
1 tablespoon tamarind water
   (see glossary)
salt, to taste
500 g (1 lb) small green
   prawns (raw shrimp), peeled
   and deveined
2 tablespoons coriander
   (cilantro) leaves, chopped

THIS DISH COMES from Little India in Singapore. The blend of fennel seeds and coconut milk gives this dish its pleasant aroma, while the tamarind water in the sauce brings out the flavour of the prawns.

Method: Heat the oil in a large saucepan. Add the mustard and fennel seeds and half the curry leaves. When the seeds start to change colour, add the onion. Sauté until the onion is soft and transparent. Now add the ginger, turmeric and chilli powder. Sauté for 1–2 minutes.
   Add the tomatoes and cook over a medium heat for 7–10 minutes, until the sauce is thick. Add the coconut and cook for 1 minute. Add the tamarind water and salt. Simmer for 2–3 minutes. Now add the prawns and cook for 4–5 minutes, until done. Check the seasoning and add more salt if necessary. Stir in the coriander and remaining curry leaves. Serve hot.

Note: Cooked and peeled prawns can also be used. If using frozen prawns, defrost before adding to the sauce. Complete the sauce and add the prawns over a low to medium heat so that they just heat through. You can replace the tamarind water with lime juice if desired.

SPICE COAST CRAB

Kekada Malabari — South India

2 tablespoons vegetable oil
1 teaspoon mustard seeds
1 teaspoon fennel seeds
2 medium onions, chopped
1 tablespoon chopped ginger
2 teaspoons red chilli powder
1 medium tomato, chopped
a few curry leaves
3 small spring onions
　　(scallions), chopped
2 teaspoons cracked black
　　peppercorns
250 g (½ lb) cooked crab meat
juice of ½ lime
salt, to taste
2 tablespoons coriander
　　(cilantro) leaves, chopped

A VERY POPULAR DISH from the Malabar (south) coast of India, a region also known as the Spice Coast because of its extensive spice plantations. The crab in this dish is usually cooked whole, but in this recipe I have used ready-cooked crab meat as it blends very well with the spices.

Method: Heat the oil in a medium frying pan or skillet. Add the mustard and fennel seeds. Add the onion and sauté until soft. Add the ginger and chilli powder. Sauté for 1 minute. Add the tomato and cook over a medium heat for about 5 minutes, until the sauce is thick. Now add the curry leaves, spring onions and peppercorns.

Reduce the heat and add the crab meat. Heat through gently. Add the lime juice and check the seasoning. Add salt if necessary. (The crab is usually cooked in salted water, so you should require very little extra salt.) Stir in half the coriander leaves.

Serve in crab shells as an appetiser or starter, garnished with the remaining coriander leaves.

CRAB IN THE SHELL

Poo-jaa — Thailand

250 g (½ lb) crab meat
　(reserve the crab shells)
250 g (½ lb) pork mince
　(ground pork)
2 tablespoons chopped ginger
2 tablespoons coriander
　(cilantro) leaves, chopped
4 green chilli peppers, chopped
1 tablespoon fish sauce
a few Kaffir lime leaves, torn
1 tablespoon cracked white
　peppercorns
3 eggs, beaten
rice flour, to coat the crab
　shells
oil, for deep-frying

CRABS ARE PROBABLY the most popular shellfish eaten in Southeast Asia. They are usually bought for special occasions, and the cooking methods are fairly elaborate. This recipe uses a combination of crab and pork, which blends very well with fresh coriander and ginger.

Method: Combine the crab, pork, ginger, coriander, green chillies, fish sauce, Kaffir lime leaves and peppercorns in a bowl. Mix well and set aside.

Rinse and dry the reserved crab shells. Brush them with some of the beaten egg. Fill the shells with the meat mixture. Steam in a steamer for about 20 minutes or until the mixture is firm. Remove from the steamer and allow to cool.

Dust the crab shell with the rice flour. Dip each shell in the remaining beaten egg. Deep-fry over a moderate heat until golden brown in colour.
Serve hot with salad and a spicy chilli sauce.

BABY CALAMARI (SQUID) WITH BAMBOO SHOOTS

Pyegyee Ngar Rebong — Burma

4 tablespoons sesame oil
2 medium onions, chopped
1 tablespoon ground turmeric
2 tablespoons red chilli powder
2 tablespoons chopped ginger
1 tablespoon chopped garlic
1 stalk lemon grass
1 cm (½ in.) piece of blachan,
    dry-roasted (see glossary)
4 green chilli peppers, split
    lengthways
2 large tomatoes, chopped
¾ cup (185 mL, 6 fl oz) coconut
    milk
500 g (1 lb) baby calamari
    (squid), cleaned
150 g (5 oz) bamboo shoots, cut
    into julienne (if using
    canned bamboo shoots,
    drain and rinse thoroughly
    to remove any brine)
salt, to taste

BAMBOO GROWS WILD in Burma and is used extensively in building and furniture-making. The young bamboo shoots are eaten widely throughout Southeast Asia, cooked with variety of vegetables and meat. Here is an unusual combination of baby calamari, ginger and bamboo shoots. If fresh bamboo shoots are unavailable, use the canned ones.

Method: Heat the oil in a large pan and sauté the onion until soft. Add the turmeric, chilli powder, ginger, garlic, lemon grass and blachan. Sauté for 2-3 minutes. Now add the chilli peppers and tomatoes. Sauté for a few minutes before adding the coconut milk. Bring to a fast boil, then reduce to a simmer.

Add the calamari and cook for 2–3 minutes. Add the bamboo shoots and heat through gently. Check the seasoning and adjust with salt if necessary.

CALAMARI (SQUID) IN RED CURRY
Pla Meuk Gaeng Phed — Thailand

10 dried red chilli peppers
1 tablespoon cumin seeds
2 tablespoons coriander seeds
2 tablespoons white vinegar
1 tablespoon blachan
4 tablespoons vegetable oil
2 medium onions, chopped
2 tablespoons chopped ginger
4 cups (1 L, 1³/4 imp. pints)
*   water*
1 stalk lemon grass
750 g (1¹/2 lb) calamari (squid),
*   cleaned*
2 teaspoons tamarind water
*   (see glossary)*
1 tablespoon granulated sugar
salt, to taste

SEAFOOD IS VERY POPULAR in south Asia, where most countries are bordered by bountiful oceans. In this recipe, prawns (shrimp) can be substituted for the calamari.

Method: Dry-roast the chilli peppers, cumin and coriander seeds. Grind to a fine powder in a spice or coffee grinder. Transfer to a small bowl. Add the vinegar and blachan to make a paste, using a little water if required. Set aside.

Heat the oil in a pan over a medium heat. Add the onion and sauté until transparent. Add the ginger and sauté for 3–4 minutes. Add the chilli/cumin paste and sauté for 1–2 minutes.

Reduce the heat to low and add the water and lemon grass. Simmer for 10–15 minutes. Add the calamari, tamarind water and sugar. Cook, stirring continuously for 45 minutes, until done. Check the seasoning and adjust with salt if necessary. Remove and discard the lemon grass. Serve hot with boiled rice.

SCALLOPS IN ROASTED CHILLI SAUCE

Pla Hoi Prik — Thailand

5 tablespoons vegetable oil
5–6 tablespoons sliced garlic
  cloves
500 g (1 lb) bay scallops
2 tablespoons roasted red chilli
  paste
2 tablespoons chopped
  coriander (cilantro) leaves
2 tablespoons sliced spring
  onions (scallions), green
  part only
1 tablespoon fish sauce
2 tablespoons holy basil leaves

A VERY QUICK yet delicate way of cooking seafood, this dish is popular throughout the gulf region of Thailand. The roasted chilli paste is usually made in advance and stored. Dry-roasting the chillies until they turn dark brown gives the curry its typical dark maroon colour.

Method: Heat the oil in a wok over a high heat. Add the garlic cloves and stir-fry until brown. Add the scallops and stir-fry for 1–2 minutes. Add the chilli paste and heat through. Reduce the heat and add the coriander, spring onions and fish sauce. Stir-fry for about 1 minute. Stir in the basil leaves. Serve hot with boiled rice.

POULTRY

CHICKEN IS A UNIVERSALLY popular meat because of its ready availability and relatively low cost. Although it is a very plain meat, proper cooking can turn it into a satisfying meal.

When using chicken in curries, it is usual to remove the skin before cooking. In these recipes, I have favoured chicken pieces with the bone in, as this is the preferred cut throughout Asia and is tastier than breast meat. However, if you prefer to use breast meat, you should monitor it carefully to ensure it does not become dry and tough.

Duck meat is not very popular generally in Asia, although duck eggs are much sought after in some areas. The duck recipes included here are adapted to popular regional cooking styles.

GREEN CHICKEN CURRY WITH EGGPLANT

Gaeng Puang Kai — Thailand

*500 g (1 lb) chicken thigh
   fillets (tenderloins),
   trimmed of any fat and
   skin*
4 tablespoons coconut cream
*3 tablespoons green curry paste
   (see page 130)*
*½ cup (about 60 g, 2 oz) Thai
   eggplant or fresh green peas*
2 tablespoons fish sauce
*1 tablespoon palm sugar or
   brown sugar*
salt, to taste
*2½ cups (625 mL, 1 imp. pint)
   coconut milk*
a few Kaffir lime leaves, torn
a few sweet basil leaves

ONE OF THE MOST FAMOUS of Thai dishes, green curry works extremely well with chicken, but can also be used with red meats. Thai eggplants are very small and grow in clusters. There is really no substitute for them, although green peas can be used instead for a similar visual effect. If you use large eggplants, dice them and leave the skin on.

Method: Cut each chicken thigh into 4 pieces. Heat the coconut cream in a large saucepan over a medium heat until the oil starts to separate from the cream. Add the green curry paste and cook, stirring, for 1–2 minutes. Add the chicken. Cook, stirring, for 10–12 minutes, until the chicken is well coated with the paste and is about half-cooked. Add the eggplant or green peas, fish sauce, sugar and salt. Cook, still stirring, for 5–7 more minutes. Add the coconut milk, reduce the heat to low and stir for 8–10 minutes, until the chicken is cooked. Check the seasoning and adjust with salt if necessary. Add the lime and basil leaves. Serve hot with rice.

CHICKEN WITH YOGHURT

Murgh Dahiwala — Punjab

2 whole chickens, 1.2–1.3 kg
    (2½–2¾ lb) each, jointed
    and trimmed of any fat
    and skin
plain (all-purpose) flour,
    seasoned with salt and
    pepper, for dusting
6 tablespoons vegetable oil
2 bay leaves
2 whole cardamom pods
2 medium onions, sliced
2 tablespoons chopped ginger
2 tablespoons chopped garlic
2 teaspoons ground turmeric
⅔ cup (150 g, 5 oz) plain
    yoghurt
salt, to taste
1 tablespoon crushed coriander
    seeds
1 tablespoon chopped green
    chilli pepper
1 tablespoon dried fenugreek
    leaves
2 tablespoons chopped
    coriander (cilantro) leaves
¾ cup (185 mL, 6 fl oz) single
    (light) cream

THE FARMING COUNTRY of India, the great tablelands of the Punjab, gave birth to this dish. In a region famous for its prized cattle and dairy products, every household has its own recipe for *Murgh Dahiwala*, but this is the one I like best.

Method: Cut the chicken into small pieces and dust in the seasoned flour. Heat 4 tablespoons of the vegetable oil in a frying pan or skillet. Add the chicken and sauté until sealed on all sides. Remove from the pan and set aside.

Heat the remaining oil in a large clean saucepan. Add the bay leaves and cardamom. Sauté for 1 minute. Add the onion and sauté until the onion is soft. Add the ginger, garlic and turmeric and sauté for a further 3–5 minutes.

Whisk the yoghurt into the onion mixture and add salt if necessary. Bring to the boil, stirring continuously. Add the chicken, reduce the heat and simmer for 15–20 minutes, until the chicken is cooked. Add the coriander seeds, chilli pepper, fenugreek and coriander. Pour in the cream and stir through. Simmer for a further 2–3 minutes. Serve immediately.

CHICKEN WITH CHILLI VINEGAR AND PICKLED CABBAGE

Kao Mok Gai — Thailand

1 whole chicken, 1–1.25 kg
(2–2½ lb), cut into 8 pieces
salt, to taste
4 tablespoons vegetable oil
1½ tablespoons red chilli
powder
1 tablespoon ground cumin
1 tablespoon ground coriander
3 bay leaves
2 medium onions, chopped
2 tablespoons chopped ginger
1 tablespoon chopped garlic
2 teaspoons ground turmeric
2 cups (300 g, 10 oz) jasmine or
other long-grain rice
1 tablespoon cracked black
peppercorns
3½ cups (875 mL, 28 fl oz)
water
2 tablespoons chopped
coriander (cilantro) leaves

CHILLI VINEGAR
2 red or green chilli peppers,
chopped
pinch of salt
pinch of sugar
¼ cup (60 mL, 2 fl oz) white
vinegar

A THAI ADAPTATION of a unique biryani from India. Unlike the Indian version, it is not served with the traditional yoghurt, but with chilli vinegar and pickled cabbage. I have used chicken in this recipe, but beef or lamb works equally well.

Method: Place the chicken in a bowl. Add the salt, 1 tablespoon of the oil, 3 teaspoons of the chilli powder, 2 teaspoons of the cumin and 2 teaspoons of the coriander. Coat the chicken thoroughly and leave to marinate for 1 hour.

Heat the remaining oil in a large saucepan over a medium heat. Quickly cook the chicken until browned on all sides. Remove and set aside.

Add the bay leaves and onion to the same pan. Sauté until the onion is transparent. Add the ginger, garlic and turmeric, and the remaining chilli powder, cumin and coriander. Sauté for 1–2 minutes. Add the rice and peppercorns. Cook, stirring, until all the rice is coated with oil.

Add the water and bring to a fast boil. Reduce the heat and simmer for 8–10 minutes. When the water has almost evaporated, add the chicken. Stir through gently, until the chicken is embedded in the rice. Cover the pan with a lid and cook for 10–12 minutes, until the rice is done.

Remove the lid and turn off the heat. Allow the dish to rest for 10–15 minutes. Before serving, fluff the rice with a chopstick or roasting fork, taking care not to mash the rice. Sprinkle with the coriander leaves. Serve hot with the chilli vinegar and Korean pickled cabbage (*kim chi*, see glossary).

Chilli vinegar: Combine the chilli peppers, salt, sugar and vinegar in a bowl. Set aside until ready to use.

CHICKEN AND YOGHURT WITH CARDAMOM AND GINGER

Murgh Dalooli Korma — Pakistan

5 cups (1.25 L, 2 imp. pints)
    water
salt, to taste
2 whole chickens, about 1.1 kg
    (2¼ lb) each, skin removed
    and each cut into 8 pieces
4 tablespoons ghee or vegetable
    oil
5 cm (2 in.) piece of cinnamon
    stick
2 medium onions, chopped
2 teaspoons ground turmeric
1½ cups (275 g, 12 oz) plain
    yoghurt
2 teaspoons ground cardamom
1 tablespoon ground ginger

THE NORTH-WEST FRONTIER province of Pakistan, famous for its fierce fighting tribes and simple yet tasty barbecued food, provides this recipe. The use of ground ginger blended with ground cardamom gives this simple meal its complex flavour.

Method: Bring 4 cups (1 L, 1¾ imp. pints) of the water to the boil. Add salt and drop the chicken pieces into the boiling water. Blanch until the flesh turns white. Remove the chicken and place in a colander or sieve. Set aside to air-dry.

Heat the ghee or vegetable oil in a saucepan. Add the cinnamon. When it starts to change colour, add the onion and sauté until the onion is transparent.

Whisk the yoghurt until smooth and silky. Add the yoghurt and turmeric to the onion mixture. Bring to the boil, stirring continuously. Add the remaining water. Reduce the heat and simmer for 8–10 minutes, until the sauce thickens. Add the chicken and cook over a medium heat for 10–15 minutes, until nearly done. Reduce the heat to low. Add the cardamom and ginger. Cook for a further 2–3 minutes to allow the flavour of the spices to blend. Serve immediately.

CHICKEN PISTACHIO

Juje Pistachio — Iran

6 tablespoons butter
2 medium onions, chopped
2 tablespoons chopped ginger
1 tablespoon chopped garlic
2 teaspoons ground turmeric
500 g (1 lb) chicken thigh
   fillets (tenderloins), diced
2 teaspoons freshly ground
   black pepper
salt, to taste
3 tablespoons pistachio nuts,
   blanched
a little water
¾ cup (185 mL, 6 fl oz) single
   (light) cream
2 tablespoons chopped
   coriander (cilantro) leaves
1 teaspoon ground green
   cardamom

THIS VERY UNUSUAL RECIPE comes from Iran, the largest producer and exporter of pistachio nuts in the world, and home of the Persian cuisine that has so influenced northern Indian food. This cuisine relies on a combination of dried fruit and cream or yoghurt to yield rich and creamy, yet subtle, flavours.

Method: Heat 3 tablespoons of the butter in a large pan over a medium heat. Add the onion and sauté until soft and transparent. Add the ginger and garlic. Sauté for 1–2 minutes. Remove from the heat and allow to cool. Transfer to a blender or food processor. Blend into a smooth purée.

Heat the remaining butter in a large saucepan. Add the onion purée. Sauté for 2–3 minutes. Add the ground turmeric and sauté for a further 1–2 minutes. Add the chicken, black pepper and salt. Cook, stirring, for 3–5 minutes, then reduce the heat to a simmer and cook for a further 8–10 minutes.

Meanwhile, purée half of the pistachio nuts with a little water (use as little water as possible) in a blender or food processor. Stir this into the chicken mixture. Add the cream and simmer for about 5 minutes, until the chicken is cooked. Add the remaining pistachio nuts, half the coriander and the ground green cardamom. Stir thoroughly. Serve immediately, garnished with the remaining coriander leaves.

CARAMELISED CHICKEN WITH GINGER AND CORIANDER (CILANTRO)

Ga Xao Gung — Vietnam

8 (875 g, 1¾ lb) chicken thigh
fillets (tenderloins)
1 tablespoon chopped ginger
1 tablespoon chopped garlic
3 tablespoons fish sauce
3 tablespoons vegetable oil
2 tablespoons caramelised
sugar (see below)
2 teaspoons cracked black
peppercorns
1 tablespoon chopped coriander
(cilantro) leaves
2 spring onions (scallions),
chopped
a few red chilli peppers,
chopped (optional)

CARAMELISED SUGAR GIVES this dish a very glossy finish. Make sure the caramel is golden brown in colour, and not burnt.

Method: Cut the chicken thighs into two across the thigh if using large ones; leave whole if using small ones. Place the chicken thighs in a bowl with the ginger, garlic and fish sauce. Leave to marinate for about 1 hour.

Heat the vegetable oil in a wok or frying pan or skillet over a medium heat. Add the chicken and its marinade. Stir-fry for 10–12 minutes, until the chicken is nearly done. Add the caramelised sugar, black peppercorns, coriander and spring onions. Stir fry for 1–2 minutes, until the chicken is well coated with the pan juices. Serve hot, garnished with the chopped red chilli peppers (if using).

Caramelised sugar: Put 2 tablespoons of sugar and ¾ cup (185 mL, 6 fl oz) of water in a saucepan. Bring to the boil. When the sugar starts to colour, reduce the heat and simmer, stirring continuously, until the syrup is dark brown. Remove from the heat and add another ¾ cup (185 mL, 6 fl oz) of water and a squeeze of lemon juice. Stir thoroughly and return to the heat. Simmer for a minute or two, then remove from the heat once again. Use as required.

LAMPRIES CURRY

Lampries — Sri Lanka

125 g (¼ lb) piece of boneless
   beef
125 g (¼ lb) piece of lamb
   shoulder (boneless shoulder
   roast)
1 tablespoon cracked black
   peppercorns
4 bay leaves
water, to cover
125 g (¼ lb) piece of pork
   shoulder
125 g (¼ lb) chicken thigh
   fillets (tenderloins)
4 tablespoons vegetable oil
3 large onions, chopped
2 tablespoons chopped ginger
1 tablespoon chopped garlic
2 tablespoons Ceylon curry
   powder (see page 133)
5 cm (2 in.) piece of cinnamon
   stick
a few curry leaves
1 stalk lemon grass
2 cups (500 mL, 16 fl oz)
   coconut milk
1 teaspoon ground cardamom
   salt, to taste

A FESTIVE DISH from Sri Lanka, this curry is a rare combination of four meats simmered in coconut milk. Unlike many south Asian curries, Lampries combines lemon grass and curry leaves to achieve its unique flavour.

Method: Combine the beef, lamb, a few peppercorns and 1 of the bay leaves in a large, heavy saucepan. Add enough water to cover and bring to the boil. Add the pork and reduce the heat to a simmer. After 10 minutes, add the chicken. Cook for 10–15 minutes, until all the meats are nearly done. Remove from the heat and set aside to cool.

Heat the vegetable oil in large saucepan. Add the remaining bay leaves and the onion. Sauté until the onion is soft. Now add the ginger, garlic, curry powder, cinnamon, curry leaves and lemon grass. Sauté for 2–3 minutes. Add the coconut milk and simmer for 8–10 minutes.

Remove all the cooled meat from the pan and dice into 1 cm (½ in.) pieces. Add to the curry mixture and simmer for about 20 minutes, or until tender. Check the seasoning and adjust with salt if necessary. Sprinkle with the ground cardamom and serve immediately.

CHICKEN CURRY WITH TAMARIND

Ayam Genting — Malaysia

*625 g (1¼ lb) chicken thigh
    fillets (tenderloins), diced*
salt, to taste
1 cm (½ in.) piece of blachan
2 tablespoons chopped ginger
1 tablespoon chopped garlic
1 tablespoon ground turmeric
1 stalk lemon grass
2 tablespoons red chilli powder
*2 tablespoons peanuts, dry-
    roasted*
4 tablespoons vegetable oil
*1²/₃ cups (400 mL, 13 fl oz)
    coconut milk*
1 tablespoon tamarind pulp
*2 tablespoons chopped
    coriander (cilantro) leaves*

I TRIED THIS DISH while travelling around Penang. A blend of Tamil and Malay cuisines, it combines peanuts (Tamil) with blachan (Malay).

Method: Rub the chicken with salt and set aside. Dry-roast the blachan in a pan until heated through. Put the blachan, ginger, garlic, ground turmeric, lemon grass, red chilli powder and peanuts into a blender or food processor. Blend or process, using a little of the vegetable oil to facilitate blending.

Heat the remaining vegetable oil in a saucepan over a medium heat. Add the blended mixture and sauté for 2–3 minutes. Add the chicken and stir-fry for 5–7 minutes. Reduce the heat to low. Add the coconut milk and tamarind pulp. Cover the pan with a lid and cook for 10–12 minutes, until nearly done. Remove the lid and increase the heat to reduce and thicken the sauce. Serve immediately, garnished with the coriander.

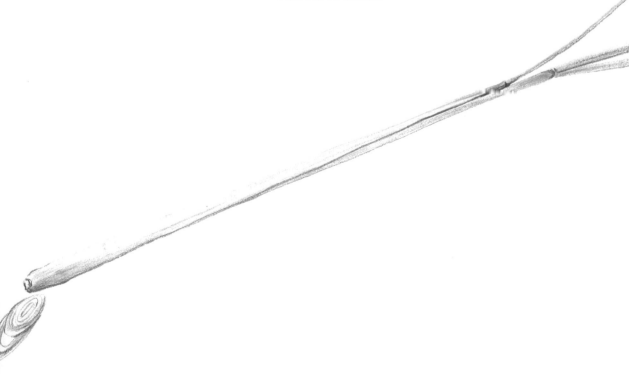

CHICKEN CURRY WITH SOY SAUCE

Kyetha Hin — Burma

4 tablespoons sesame oil
3 bay leaves
5 cm (2 in.) piece of cinnamon
   stick
2 medium onions, chopped
4 green chilli peppers
2 tablespoons chopped ginger
2 tablespoons chopped garlic
4 tablespoons curry powder
1 cm (½ in.) piece of blachan
12 pieces chicken, about
   125 g (¼ lb) each
2 tablespoons soy sauce
1 cup (250 mL, 8 fl oz) water

EVERY COUNTRY IN THE WORLD probably has a recipe for chicken curry. Some like it very spicy; some like it with fruit. In Burma, they like it with a bit of soy sauce.

Method: Heat the sesame oil in a saucepan over a medium heat. Add the bay leaves and cinnamon stick. When they start to change colour, after about 1 minute, add the onion. Sauté until the onion is soft. Add the chilli peppers, ginger, garlic, curry powder and blachan. Sauté for 2–3 minutes, then add the chicken.

Stir-fry the chicken until it is sealed on all sides. Add the soy sauce and water. Cover the pan with a lid and cook for 10–12 minutes, until the chicken is nearly done. Remove the lid and continue cooking for 3–5 minutes, to allow the sauce to reduce and thicken slightly. Serve hot.

SPICY CHICKEN WINGS

Murgh Pankh — Bhutan

20 (875 g, 1¾ lb) chicken wings
1 tablespoon ground turmeric
2 tablespoons chilli powder
2 teaspoons mustard powder
2 tablespoons chopped ginger
2 tablespoons soy sauce
2 tablespoons chopped
*   coriander (cilantro) leaves*
2 teaspoons brown sugar
1 egg
¾ cup (100 g, 3 oz) plain
*   (all-purpose) flour*
vegetable oil, for frying
extra coriander (cilantro)
*   leaves, to garnish*

CHICKEN WINGS ARE perfect finger food with pre-dinner drinks or at a cocktail party. They are easy to prepare and fast to cook. Here is a recipe from Bhutan, which is very simple yet full of flavour.

Method: Place the chicken wings in a bowl. Add the ground turmeric, chilli powder, mustard powder, ginger, soy sauce, coriander and sugar. Mix thoroughly.

Whisk the egg and add it to the chicken mixture. Add the flour, mixing until the wings are well coated. Marinate in the refrigerator for 3–4 hours.

Heat the vegetable oil in a deep-fryer or deep saucepan over a moderate heat. Drop in the chicken wings and cook for 10–12 minutes, until golden brown. Remove from the oil and drain on paper towels (absorbent kitchen paper). Serve hot, garnished with the extra coriander.

CHICKEN AND POTATO CURRY

Kyetha Aloo Hin — Burma

*16 pieces chicken, about 1 kg
    (2 lb) total weight
2 tablespoons ground turmeric
salt, to taste
4 tablespoons vegetable oil
2 medium onions, chopped
2 tablespoons chopped ginger
2 tablespoons chopped garlic
3 tablespoons red chilli powder
8 small new potatoes, peeled
2 cups (500 mL, 16 fl oz) water
2 tablespoons fish sauce
2 tablespoons chopped
    coriander (cilantro) leaves*

UNLIKE WESTERN CUISINE, which is often stock-based, most Eastern cuisine is based on water. Water and spices blend to give curries their individual tastes. The fish sauce and the spices in this dish blend to give this light chicken curry its flavour.

Method: Place the chicken in a medium bowl. Add the ground turmeric and salt. Mix thoroughly and set aside.

Heat the vegetable oil in a large saucepan. Add the onion and sauté until transparent. Add the ginger and garlic. Sauté for 1–2 minutes. Add the chilli powder, then the chicken and its marinade. Stir fry for 3–5 minutes, until the chicken is sealed on all sides. Add the potatoes and mix into the curry. Add the water and fish sauce. Bring to a fast boil, then reduce the heat to low. Cover the pan with a lid and simmer for 15–20 minutes, until the chicken and potatoes are cooked through. Stir in the coriander and serve immediately. This fairly thin curry goes best with boiled rice.

SLICED CHICKEN WITH HOLY BASIL

Phad Pik Gai — Thailand

3 tablespoons sesame oil
2 teaspoons chopped garlic
1 tablespoon chopped ginger
1 tablespoon chopped red chilli
    peppers
500 g (1 lb) chicken thigh
    fillets (tenderloins),
    trimmed of any fat and
    skin, and sliced
2 tablespoons soy sauce
2 tablespoons water
2 teaspoons brown sugar
3 tablespoons holy basil or
    ordinary basil leaves
4 spring onions (scallions),
    green part only, sliced

ANOTHER BLEND OF CHINESE stir-fry techniques with the addition of holy basil from India. In India, this plant is associated with Hindu ceremonies and festivals. It is revered by the Hindus and is popular as a medicinal herb. Ordinary basil or even mint leaves can be substituted.

Method: Heat the sesame oil in a wok over a medium heat. Add the garlic, ginger and red chilli peppers. Stir-fry for 3–5 minutes. Add the chicken and stir-fry for 3–5 minutes, until the chicken is sealed on all sides. Stir in the soy sauce, water and sugar. Cook for about 5 minutes, until done. Add the basil and spring onions. Serve immediately.

DRY CHICKEN CURRY

Kyetha See Byan — Burma

4 tablespoons soy sauce
*2 tablespoons garlic, chopped
    and puréed*
*3 tablespoons ginger, chopped
    and puréed*
*2 tablespoons (soft) brown
    sugar*
*2 teaspoons ground white
    pepper*
1 tablespoon ground coriander
1 tablespoon red chilli powder
*16 pieces chicken, about 1 kg
    (2 lb) total weight*

THIS EASY-TO-COOK DISH is perfect for a Sunday barbecue. The bones are left in the chicken, which means it cooks fairly quickly.

Method: Combine the soy sauce, garlic, ginger, brown sugar, white pepper, ground coriander and chilli powder in a large bowl. Whisk thoroughly. Add the chicken and marinate at room temperature for 3–4 hours — no longer.

Remove the chicken from the marinade and cook over a medium heat on the barbecue or under the griller (broiler), turning occasionally, until done. Serve hot with a salad or rice.

CHICKEN COOKED WITH POTATO AND ONION

Kar Lee — Thailand

4 tablespoons coconut cream
4 tablespoons green curry paste
   (see page 130)
12 pieces (875 g, 1³/₄ lb) chicken
4 medium potatoes, quartered
2 ½ cups (625 mL, 1 imp. pint)
   coconut milk
2 tablespoons fish sauce
1 tablespoon palm or brown
   sugar
a few Kaffir lime leaves, torn
1 medium onion, sliced
salt, to taste

THIS RECIPE COMES from southern Thailand, where the population is largely Muslim and the influence of Mogul cuisine is easily apparent. Though southern Thai curries are fairly simple compared to the complexities of later Mogul cuisine, basic similarities do exist. Here, the onions are added during the final stages of cooking so that they remain crunchy and firm.

Method: Heat the coconut cream in a large saucepan over a medium heat until the oil starts to separate from the cream. Add the curry paste and cook for 3–5 minutes. Now add the chicken pieces. Stir-fry for about 5 minutes, until the chicken is coated with the paste. Add the potatoes and cook for 1–2 minutes, then add the coconut milk, fish sauce, palm sugar and lime leaves. Bring to a fast boil. Reduce the heat and cook for 15–20 minutes, until nearly done. Stir in the onion and heat through, taking care not to break up the potatoes. Check the seasoning and add salt if necessary. Serve immediately.

CHICKEN CAFREAL

Kori Cafreal — Goa

2 chickens, 1.2–1.3 kg
   (2½–2¾ lb) each, cut into
   halves, or 4 spatchcocks
   (Cornish game hens)
salt, to taste
6 black peppercorns, crushed
2 teaspoons cumin seeds
1 tablespoon coriander seeds
3 green (small) cardamom
   pods
3 whole cloves
2 cm (1 in.) piece of cinnamon
   stick
2 tablespoons chopped ginger
2 tablespoons chopped garlic
2 tablespoons chopped
   coriander (cilantro) leaves
4 green chilli peppers, chopped
a little white vinegar
vegetable oil, for frying

AN INDIANISED VERSION of roast chicken, this spicy dish can be made with either young or mature chickens. If cooking for a large number of people, you may prefer to use chicken pieces. The dish goes very well with boiled rice or a potato salad.

Method: Rub the chicken halves or spatchcocks with salt. Set aside.

Dry-roast the black peppercorns, cumin and coriander seeds, cardamom pods, cloves and cinnamon in a heavy saucepan, until fragrant. Grind to a powder in a spice or coffee grinder. Transfer to a blender or food processor. Add the ginger, garlic, coriander leaves, chilli peppers, white vinegar (use as little vinegar as possible) and blend to a thick paste. Rub the paste all over the chicken or spatchcock. Leave to marinate for 1–2 hours.

Preheat the griller (broiler) to medium hot. Alternatively, preheat the oven to 180°C (350°F/gas mark 4).

Heat the vegetable oil in a large frying pan or skillet over a medium heat. Shallow-fry the chicken or spatchcock until sealed on all sides. Remove and finish cooking under the griller or in the oven for 15–20 minutes. Cooking time will depend on the thickness of the pieces. Serve hot.

Tip: You can make a sauce of the pan drippings as an accompaniment to the poultry. Simply make a paste with a little water and cornflour (cornstarch). Add to the pan drippings and heat, stirring continuously, until a thick sauce forms.

CHICKEN CURRY WITH LEMON GRASS

Gaeng Gai — Thailand

6 whole red chilli peppers
1 tablespoon chopped galangal
10 white peppercorns, crushed
1 tablespoon chopped garlic
2 teaspoons coriander seeds
1 tablespoon blachan
1 tablespoon chopped coriander
    (cilantro) root
2 stalks lemon grass
a little water
4 tablespoons vegetable oil
12 chicken thigh fillets
    (tenderloins) (875 g, 1¾ lb)
1¼ cups (300 mL, 10 fl oz)
    water
2 tablespoons fish sauce
8 Kaffir lime leaves, torn
salt, to taste
1 tablespoon sliced spring
    onion (scallion)

THIS ROBUST, MEDIUM-SPICED dish is from northern Thailand. The addition of lemon grass and Kaffir lime leaves towards the end of the cooking imparts a vigorous flavour. Though best served with rice, it also goes well with crusty bread.

Method: Combine the chilli peppers, galangal, white peppercorns, garlic, coriander seeds, blachan, coriander root and 1 stalk of the lemon grass in a blender or food processor. Add just enough water to make a paste and blend or process until smooth.

Heat the vegetable oil in a saucepan over a medium heat. Add the paste and sauté for 1–2 minutes. Add the chicken pieces and stir-fry for 5–8 minutes, until the chicken is well coated with the paste. Now add the water and fish sauce. Cook for 15–20 minutes, until the chicken is done.

Add the remaining lemon grass and the Kaffir lime leaves. Check the seasoning and add salt if necessary. Serve hot, garnished with the spring onion.

CHICKEN WITH CARDAMOM

Murgh Elaichi — Punjab

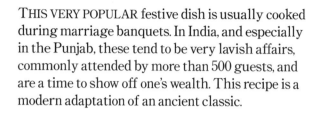

12 chicken thighs (still on the
  bone), (875 g, 1¾ lb)
  trimmed of any fat and
  skin
salt, to taste
6 tablespoons ghee or vegetable
  oil
plain (all-purpose) flour, for
  dusting
2 bay leaves
2 whole cardamom pods
1 tablespoon crushed coriander
  seeds
2 medium onions, chopped
1 tablespoon chopped ginger
1 tablespoon chopped garlic
1¾ cups (450 mL, 14 fl oz)
  coconut milk
4 green chilli peppers
1 tablespoon ground green
  cardamom (see note)
1 tablespoon cracked black
  pepper
2 tablespoons chopped
  coriander (cilantro) leaves
salt, to taste

THIS VERY POPULAR festive dish is usually cooked
during marriage banquets. In India, and especially
in the Punjab, these tend to be very lavish affairs,
commonly attended by more than 500 guests, and
are a time to show off one's wealth. This recipe is a
modern adaptation of an ancient classic.

Method: Rub the chicken thighs with salt. Set aside.
    Heat 4 tablespoons of the ghee or vegetable oil
in a large saucepan. Dust the chicken in the flour,
transfer to the saucepan and sauté for 2–3 minutes.
Do not allow the chicken to brown.
    Remove the chicken pieces and set aside.
Heat the remaining oil in the same pan. Add the bay
leaves, cardamom pods and coriander seeds. Sauté for
1–2 minutes. Add the onion and sauté until the onion
is soft. Add the ginger and garlic paste. Sauté for a
further 1–2 minutes. Return the chicken to the pan.
Add the coconut milk and chilli peppers. Bring to a
fast boil, then reduce the heat to low. Cover the pan
with a lid and simmer for 15–20 minutes, until the
chicken is cooked. Remove the lid and add the
ground green cardamom, black pepper and
coriander. Check the seasoning and add salt if
necessary. Serve hot with rice or crusty bread.

Ground green cardamom: Dry-roast several green
(small) cardamom pods in a frying pan or skillet.
Place in a spice or coffee grinder and grind to a
powder. Use as required. Store any leftover ground
cardamom in an airtight jar.

CHICKEN COORGI

Murgh Coorgi— Coorg

4 tablespoons vegetable oil

2 bay leaves

4 whole cardamom pods

2 medium onions, chopped

2 tablespoons chopped ginger

3 cloves garlic, chopped

2 medium tomatoes, chopped

450 g (14 oz) chicken thigh
fillets (tenderloins),
trimmed of any fat and
skin

1 tablespoon chopped green
chilli pepper

1 tablespoon crushed dried red
chilli pepper

1 tablespoon crushed coriander
seeds

2 teaspoons fenugreek leaves

¾ cup (185 mL, 6 fl oz) coconut
milk

1 tablespoon whole green
peppercorns

1 tablespoon chopped coriander
(cilantro) leaves

THIS DISH IS AN UNUSUAL blend of tomatoes, coconut and pepper from the far south of India. Spicy foods like this are favoured in hot areas for their ability to make you perspire.

Method: Heat the vegetable oil in a large saucepan. Add the bay leaves and cardamom pods. Stir through quickly before adding the onion. Sauté until the onion is transparent. Add half the ginger and the garlic. Sauté for 1–2 minutes. Add the tomatoes. Bring to the boil, then reduce the heat to medium. Simmer for 7–10 minutes, until the sauce thickens.

Cut each thigh fillet into four. Add to the sauce and cook over a medium heat for 10–15 minutes, until nearly done. Add the remaining ginger, red and green chilli peppers, coriander seeds, fenugreek leaves, coconut cream and green peppercorns. Simmer for a further 5 minutes.

Stir thoroughly. Serve immediately, garnished with the coriander.

SPICY DUCK CURRY

Bairthar Hin — Burma

1 duck, 1.6–1.8 kg (3–3½ lb), trimmed of any fat and skin, and cut into small pieces
2 tablespoons chopped ginger
2 tablespoons chopped garlic
salt, to taste
2 tablespoons white vinegar
4 tablespoons peanut or vegetable oil
3 medium onions, chopped
2 tablespoons ground cumin
2 tablespoons ground coriander
3 tablespoons red chilli powder
3 medium tomatoes, chopped
2 cups (500 mL, 16 fl oz) water
4 tablespoons fish sauce
2 tablespoons ground white pepper
2 tablespoons chopped coriander (cilantro) leaves

FREE-RANGE DUCK is very popular as a dish for special occasions in the cuisines of Southeast Asia. When used in a curry, the duck is usually skinned before cooking.

Method: Place the duck pieces in a bowl. In a separate bowl combine 1 tablespoon of the ginger, 1 tablespoon of the garlic, the salt and the vinegar. Rub the duck thoroughly with the mixture. Leave to marinate for about 1 hour.

Meanwhile, heat the peanut or vegetable oil in a large saucepan over a low heat. Add the onion and sauté until soft, then add the remaining ginger and garlic. Sauté for 2–3 minutes. Add the ground cumin, ground coriander and red chilli powder. Sauté for 2–3 minutes. Increase the heat to medium, add the tomato and cook for 8–10 minutes.

Add the duck and its marinade. Cook, stirring, until the duck is evenly coated in the mixture. Add the water, fish sauce and white pepper. Bring to a fast boil, then reduce the heat to a simmer. Cover the pan with a lid and cook for 10–15 minutes, stirring occasionally, until nearly done. Remove the lid to finish off cooking. Sprinkle with the coriander leaves. The sauce should now be fairly thick. If not, remove the meat from the pan, return the sauce to the heat and simmer until it reduces in volume. Return the duck to the pan and heat through gently. Serve hot with rice or bread.

PENANG DUCK CURRY

Gaeng Tianya — Thailand

*1 Chinese barbecued duck or
   roast duck (available from
   Oriental butchers or
   specialist poultry suppliers)*
*¼ cup (60 mL, 2 fl oz) coconut
   cream*
*3 tablespoons red curry paste
   (see page 131)*
a few Kaffir lime leaves
*½ cup (about 60 g, 2 oz) Thai
   eggplant or fresh green peas*
1 tablespoon fish sauce
*1 tablespoon palm or brown
   sugar*
*1½ cups (375 mL, 12 fl oz)
   coconut milk*
salt, to taste
a few basil leaves

ANOTHER UNIQUE BLEND of two cuisines. In this recipe, Chinese-style barbecued duck combines with Thai red curry paste. This is a thick curry in which the duck is liberally coated with the paste.

Method: Cut the roast duck into serving-size pieces. If buying Chinese barbecued duck, ask the butcher to do this for you.

Heat the coconut cream in a large saucepan over a medium heat, stirring occasionally, until the oil separates from the cream. Add the red curry paste and cook, stirring, for 1–2 minutes. Add the Kaffir lime leaves and Thai eggplant or green peas. Cook, stirring, for a further 1–2 minutes. Add the fish sauce, sugar, coconut milk and roast duck. Cook over a low heat until the duck warms through. Check the seasoning and add salt if necessary. Stir in the basil. Serve immediately with boiled rice.

RANGOON ROAST DUCK

Batek Roast — Burma

2 tablespoons sesame oil
3 tablespoons soy sauce
2 tablespoons chopped ginger
2 tablespoons chopped garlic
2 tablespoons malt vinegar
2 medium onions, diced
a few black peppercorns
a few coriander seeds
1 level teaspoon cumin seeds
2 medium tomatoes, diced
1 whole duck, 1.6–1.8 kg
   (3–3½ lb)
a little water
2 tablespoons cornflour
   (cornstarch)

THIS MULTINATIONAL RECIPE comes from the Rangoon Club, a colonial club built for the British 'gentry'. The chefs were great innovators, especially when it came to fusing cuisines. In this recipe, we find Indian, Chinese and Western influences.

Method: Combine the sesame oil, soy sauce, ginger, garlic and vinegar in a large bowl. Place the duck in the bowl. Coat with the marinade and allow to marinate at room temperature for 1–2 hours.

Preheat the oven to 240°–260°C (475°–500°F/gas mark 9–10). Place the onion, black peppercorns, coriander and cumin seeds and tomatoes in a roasting pan. Lay the duck on top and roast in the oven for 45–50 minutes, until done, basting frequently with the dripping fat.

When cooked, remove the duck from the pan. Skim off the fat, strain the remaining liquid and pour into a small saucepan. Bring to the boil. Mix a little water with the cornflour to make a thin paste. Add to the boiling liquid and whisk until the sauce thickens. It should be smooth and slightly thick. Serve the duck hot, accompanied by the sauce and some crusty bread.

DUCK WITH GREEN CHILLI
Babek Kelia — Indonesia

*10 medium green chilli
   peppers, sliced
2 medium onions, chopped
1 tablespoon ground turmeric
2 tablespoons ground coriander
3 tablespoons raw cashew nuts
1 tablespoon ground ginger
4 tablespoons chopped garlic
a few black peppercorns
a little water
4 tablespoons peanut oil
2 bay leaves
1 stalk lemon grass, sliced and
   bruised (see glossary)
1 whole duck, about 1.7 kg
   (3¼ lb), jointed
a pinch of shrimp powder
1 cup (250 mL, 8 fl oz) water
1 tablespoon tamarind pulp*

DUCK IS A FESTIVE dish throughout most of
Southeast Asia. It should be cooked beforehand and
then reheated, if possible — it tastes much better
that way.

*Method:*Combine the chilli peppers, onion, ground
turmeric, ground coriander, cashew nuts, ground
ginger, garlic and black peppercorns in a blender or
food processor. Add a little water (use as little water
as possible) and blend to a paste. Set aside.

Heat the peanut oil in a large pan over a medium
heat. Add the bay leaves, lemon grass and paste.
Sauté for 4–5 minutes. Add the duck and shrimp
powder. Cook, stirring, until the duck is sealed on
all sides. Add the water and cook over a low heat
for 15–20 minutes, until the duck is almost done.
Remove from the heat and set aside until ready to
serve. Before serving, skim off any excess fat, add the
tamarind pulp and heat through gently. Serve hot.

LAMB

LAMB AND GOAT meat are very popular in inland India, with lamb being reared mainly in the upper regions of the sub-continent and goat proving popular towards the plains.

In lamb dishes, shoulder meat tends to turn out much tastier and more tender than other joints. And it should be free of excess fat, as a fatty joint will overpower the flavours in a curry.

All the recipes given here use lamb, but if you wish to use goat meat, extend the cooking time until the meat becomes tender. Another way of tenderising goat meat is to marinate it first with some of the dry spices and salt.

LAMB WITH CHILLI

Gosht Mirchi Korma — Kashmir

4 Kashmiri chilli peppers
    or 1 large red capsicum
    (bell pepper)
4 small red chilli peppers, seeds
    removed
2 teaspoons fennel seeds
4 green cardamom pods
2 black (whole) cardamom
    pods
1 medium onion, chopped
1 tablespoon chopped garlic
2 tablespoons chopped ginger
a little water
4 tablespoons ghee or vegetable
    oil
500 g (1 lb) lean lamb, cut into
    1 cm (½ in.) cubes
salt, to taste
1¼ cups (300 mL, 10 fl oz)
    water
2 tablespoons tamarind water
    (see glossary)
2 tablespoons chopped
    coriander (cilantro) leaves

THE VALLEY OF KASHMIR is the home of this dish, in which chilli peppers form the main ingredient. The chillies used are a mix of large red ones for colour and small ones for heat. The sauce is fairly thin, but quite spicy — not for the faint-hearted. If Kashmiri chilli peppers are not available, use a red capsicum (bell pepper) instead.

Method: Dry-roast the Kashmiri chilli peppers or capsicum, red chilli peppers, fennel seeds and cardamom pods in a heavy saucepan for 3–5 minutes, until fragrant. Grind to a powder in a spice or coffee grinder.

Transfer the powder to an electric blender or food processor. Add the onion, garlic and ginger. Blend or process into a paste, adding as little water as possible.

Heat the ghee or vegetable oil in a large saucepan over a medium heat. Add the paste and sauté for 4–5 minutes. Add the lamb and stir-fry until the meat is completely coated with the paste. Add the salt and water. Bring to a fast boil, then reduce the heat and simmer for 20–25 minutes. When the lamb is nearly done, add the tamarind water and check the seasoning. Add more salt if necessary. When the lamb is cooked, stir in the coriander leaves. Remove from the heat and serve immediately.

LAMB KORMA

Gosht Korma — India

500 g (1 lb) lamb, trimmed of
    any fat and sinew, diced
1½ tablespoons chopped ginger
1 tablespoon chopped garlic
1 stalk lemon grass
a few black peppercorns
2 teaspoons coriander seeds
1 tablespoon ground cumin
salt, to taste
5 tablespoons sesame oil
10 almonds or cashew nuts
a little water
4 bay leaves
2 medium onions, chopped
1 cup (250 mL, 8 fl oz) coconut
    milk
1 tablespoon tamarind pulp
½ tablespoon Kashmiri
    masala (see page 134)

A BLEND OF NORTHWEST and southeast Indian cuisine. Coconuts are rarely used in north India, but are one of the main ingredients in the cuisine of the southeast. In the northwest, dried fruits and nuts are used extensively as a thickener in curries — the equivalent of coconuts in the south. This recipe uses both nuts and coconut.

Method: Put the lamb in a bowl. Add the ginger, garlic, lemon grass, laos powder, black peppercorns, coriander seeds, ground cumin, salt and 2 tablespoons of the sesame oil. Mix well and leave to marinate for 30 minutes.

Grind the nuts with a little water (use as little water as possible) to make a paste. Set aside.

Heat the remaining sesame oil in a large saucepan over a medium heat. Add the bay leaves and onion. Sauté until the onion is soft, then add the marinated lamb. Cook for 5–10 minutes, stirring, until the lamb is well sealed on all sides. Reduce the heat, add the coconut milk and simmer for 15–20 minutes, until the lamb is nearly done. Add the nut paste and tamarind pulp. Cook uncovered for a further 10 minutes, until the curry thickens and coats the lamb. Remove from the heat and serve immediately

KATHA LAMB CURRY

Seikathar Hin — Burma

500 g (1 lb) lamb, cut into 1 cm (¹/₂ in.) cubes
1 tablespoon ground turmeric
2 teaspoons salt
2 tablespoons red chilli powder
3 tablespoons vegetable oil
2 medium onions, chopped
2 tablespoons chopped ginger
1 tablespoon chopped garlic
1¹/₂ tablespoons ground cumin
2 medium potatoes, cut into wedges
scant 1 cup (225 mL, 7 fl oz) water
2 tablespoons fish sauce
salt, to taste
2 tablespoons chopped coriander (cilantro) leaves

A DISH FROM the Katha region of Burma, an area of intensive rice cultivation and brimming paddy fields. Here, families usually keep goats for their milk and meat. Potatoes and other vegetables are often added to curries, which are always served with white rice.

Method: Put the lamb in a large bowl. Add the ground turmeric, salt and 1 tablespoon of the chilli powder. Mix well and leave to marinate for 10 minutes.

Heat the vegetable oil in a large saucepan over a medium heat. Add the onion and sauté until transparent. Add the ginger and garlic. Sauté for 1–2 minutes. Now add the cumin and remaining chilli powder. Reduce the heat to low and sauté for 1–2 minutes.

Add the marinated lamb and stir-fry for 3–5 minutes to brown the meat on all sides. Add the potatoes and stir-fry for a further 2 minutes, then add the water and fish sauce. Simmer for 25–30 minutes, until the lamb and potatoes are cooked. Check the seasoning and add more salt if necessary. Stir in the coriander leaves and remove from the heat. Serve hot with boiled rice.

LAMB WITH POTATOES
Shab Degh — Kashmir

4 tablespoons ghee or vegetable
  oil
3 bay leaves
2 medium onions, chopped
1 tablespoon chopped ginger
1 tablespoon chopped garlic
2 teaspoons ground turmeric
1 tablespoon red chilli powder
²/₃ cup (150 g, 5 oz) plain
  yoghurt
375 g (³/₄ lb) lean lamb, cut
  into 1 cm (¹/₂ in.) cubes
salt, to taste
2 small potatoes, quartered
2 teaspoons Kashmiri garam
  masala (see page 134)
2 tablespoons chopped
  coriander (cilantro) leaves
2 tablespoons ground ginger

THIS VERY POPULAR DISH from northwest Pakistan derives its unique flavour from the addition of ground ginger. The yoghurt combines well with the onions and spices to give the dish its beautiful rich colour.

Method: Heat the ghee or vegetable oil in a medium saucepan. Add the bay leaves and onion. Sauté until the onion is golden in colour. Add the ginger and garlic. Sauté for 3–5 minutes. Now add the ground turmeric and chilli powder. Sauté for another minute.

Meanwhile, whisk the yoghurt until smooth and silky. Stir into the onion mixture. Bring to the boil, stirring continuously. Reduce the heat, then add the lamb and salt. Cook for about 10 minutes. Add the potatoes and cook over a medium heat for 15–20 minutes, until done. Reduce the heat to low and cook for a further 10–15 minutes. Add the garam masala, coriander leaves and ground ginger. Stir through gently. Remove from the heat and serve immediately.

LAMB WITH YOGHURT

Gosht Dahiwala — Punjab

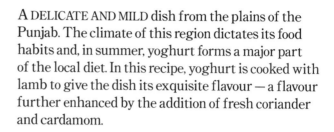

4 tablespoons vegetable oil
2 bay leaves
4 whole cloves
3 medium onions, chopped
2 tablespoons chopped ginger
1 tablespoon chopped garlic
500 g (1 lb) lamb, cut into 1 cm
   (¹⁄₂ in.) cubes
4 green chilli peppers
salt, to taste
1¹⁄₂ cups (375 g, 12 oz) plain
   yoghurt
scant ¹⁄₂ cup (100 mL, 3 fl oz)
   single (light) cream
1 tablespoon cracked white
   peppercorns
3 tablespoons chopped
   coriander (cilantro)
2 teaspoons ground cardamom
   (see note)

A DELICATE AND MILD dish from the plains of the Punjab. The climate of this region dictates its food habits and, in summer, yoghurt forms a major part of the local diet. In this recipe, yoghurt is cooked with lamb to give the dish its exquisite flavour — a flavour further enhanced by the addition of fresh coriander and cardamom.

Method: Heat the oil in a deep saucepan over a high heat. When the oil starts to smoke, reduce the heat to medium. Add the bay leaves and cloves. Sauté for 1 minute. Add the onion and sauté for a further 2 minutes, until the onion is soft and transparent. Now add the ginger and garlic. Reduce the heat to low and sauté for 2 minutes. Add the lamb, green chilli peppers and salt. Cook, stirring occasionally, for 8–10 minutes, until the lamb is sealed on all sides.

Meanwhile, whisk the yoghurt until smooth. Add to the lamb and bring the mixture to the boil, stirring continuously. Reduce the heat and simmer for 15–20 minutes, until almost cooked. Add the cream and white peppercorns. Simmer for a further 2–3 minutes. Stir in the coriander and ground cardamom. Remove from the heat and serve immediately.

Note: Freshly ground cardamom is much more aromatic than store-bought ground cardamom. If you have time, you can easily make your own. Simply place several whole cardamom pods in a heavy saucepan. Dry-roast over a very low heat for 4–5 minutes. Remove from the heat and allow to cool. Grind to a powder in a spice or coffee grinder. Any leftover powder will last for several weeks if stored in a screw-top glass jar.

SINDHI LAMB

Sayel Gosht — Pakistan

500 g (1 lb) lamb, cut into 1 cm (¹⁄₂ in.) cubes
scant ¹⁄₂ cup (100 g, 3 oz) plain yoghurt
2 medium onions, chopped
2 tablespoons ground coriander
2 teaspoons ground turmeric
1 tablespoon red chilli powder
salt, to taste
3 medium tomatoes, chopped
2 tablespoons chopped ginger
1 tablespoon chopped garlic
2 tablespoons ghee or vegetable oil
2 tablespoons chopped fresh mint
2 tablespoons chopped coriander (cilantro) leaves

THIS RECIPE ORIGINATED in the ancient Sind region of Pakistan. (The word 'Sind' comes from 'Sindhu' — the land of Indus.) Persian influence in the area dates back to the 2nd century BC, and is still reflected in its customs, language and food.

Method: Place the lamb in a bowl. Whisk the yoghurt until smooth and silky. Add to the lamb and mix thoroughly. Add the onion, ground coriander, ground turmeric, chilli powder, salt, tomatoes, ginger and garlic. Leave to marinate for 10–15 minutes.

Heat the ghee or vegetable oil in a large saucepan. Add the lamb mixture and bring to the boil. Reduce the heat to low and simmer, stirring occasionally, for 20–25 minutes, or until the lamb is tender. (If the curry becomes too dry, add a little water.) Stir in the mint and coriander leaves just before serving. Remove from the heat and serve immediately.

CHETTINAD LAMB AND COCONUT

Tengai Attu Kari — Tamil Nadu

½–1 tablespoon red chilli
    powder
1 tablespoon ground turmeric
a little water
5 tablespoons vegetable oil
2 teaspoons mustard seeds
2 medium onions, sliced
2 tablespoons ginger paste
1 tablespoon garlic paste
500 g (1 lb) lamb, cut into 1 cm
    (½ in.) cubes
1 cup (250 mL, 8 fl oz) coconut
    milk
salt, to taste
2 tablespoons tamarind water
    (see glossary)
a few curry leaves
60 g (2 oz) coconut slices or
    shredded coconut, fried in
    a little vegetable oil
2 teaspoons cracked black
    peppercorns

THE CHETTINADS ARE based in Tamil Nadu.
A traditional merchant class within India, they
are also believed to have traded with Laos, Vietnam,
Malaysia and other countries in the region since
time immemorial. Their cuisine has spread widely
throughout India, and they are among the few meat-
eaters in the otherwise predominantly vegetarian
Tamil Nadu region. This is one of their festive dishes.

Method: Mix the chilli powder and ground turmeric
with a little water to make paste. Set aside.

Heat the vegetable oil in a deep saucepan over a
medium heat. Add the mustard seeds and fry until
they start to pop. Add the onion and sauté for
4–5 minutes, until the onion is transparent. Add the
ginger and garlic pastes and sauté for 2–3 minutes.
Add the chilli paste and sauté for a further
2–3 minutes.

Now add the lamb and stir-fry for 5–7 minutes,
until the meat is sealed on all sides. Add half
the coconut milk and season with salt. Cook over
a medium heat for 15–20 minutes, until the lamb
is done.

Add the tamarind water and stir in the remaining
coconut milk, the curry leaves and half the black
peppercorns. Simmer for 2–3 minutes. Serve
immediately, garnished with the coconut slices and
the remaining black peppercorns.

LAMB WITH FIGS

Gosht Anjiri — Kashmir

4 tablespoons vegetable oil
2 bay leaves
2 medium onions, chopped
2 tablespoons chopped ginger
2 tablespoons chopped garlic
500 g (1 lb) lean lamb, cut into
   1 cm (½ in.) cubes
salt, to taste
scant ½ cup (100 g, 3 oz) plain
   yoghurt
¾ cup (100 g, 3 oz) ground
   almonds
scant ½ cup (100 mL, 3 fl oz)
   single (light) cream
1¼–1½ cups (60 g, 2 oz)
   chopped spinach
4 green chilli peppers, chopped
4 dried figs, quartered
1 teaspoon ground cardamom
2 teaspoons poppy seeds

AN OLD MOGUL RECIPE adapted to modern times. In Kashmir, the figs are sun-dried in summer and stored for use in winter.

Method: Heat the vegetable oil in a saucepan over a medium heat. Add the bay leaves and onion. Sauté until the onion is transparent. Add the ginger and garlic. Sauté for 1–2 minutes. Now add the lamb and season with salt. Stir-fry for 8–10 minutes, until the lamb is well sealed on all sides.

Whisk the yoghurt until smooth and silky. Stir into the lamb mixture. Bring to a fast boil, stirring continuously, then reduce to a simmer. Continue cooking for a further 10 minutes. (If the lamb sticks to the bottom of the pan, add a little water.)

Whisk the ground almonds into the cream until thick. Add to the lamb when it is nearly done, along with the spinach, chilli peppers, half the figs and the ground cardamom. Simmer for 1–2 minutes. Turn off the heat and allow the curry to rest in the pan for 5–8 minutes. Serve garnished with the remaining figs and the poppy seeds.

SPICY LAMB

Gosht Jalfry — India

5 tablespoons vegetable oil
2 bay leaves
2 medium onions, chopped
2 tablespoons chopped ginger
1 tablespoon chopped garlic
500 g (1 lb) lean lamb, cut into
    1 cm (½ in.) cubes
salt, to taste
4 tablespoons plain yoghurt
4 tablespoons single (light)
    cream
1 tablespoon crushed coriander
    seeds
1 tablespoon crushed red chilli
    peppers
3 green chilli peppers, chopped
2 teaspoons fenugreek leaves
1 tablespoon chopped coriander
    (cilantro) leaves

THIS IS AN ELEGANT dish from northern India. It is fairly easy to make and can be adapted to suit individual taste — mild or hot. It works equally well with beef.

Method: Heat the vegetable oil in a large saucepan over a medium heat. Add the bay leaves and onion. Sauté until the onion is soft, then add the ginger and garlic. Sauté for 1–2 minutes. Now add the lamb and salt. Stir-fry for 12–15 minutes, until the meat is well browned on all sides. (Add a little water if the lamb sticks to the bottom of the pan.)

Whisk the yoghurt and cream together. Slowly add this to the lamb, stirring continuously so that the sauce does not curdle. When the sauce starts to thicken, reduce the heat and add the coriander seeds, red and green chilli peppers and fenugreek leaves. Serve hot, garnished with the coriander leaves.

MOGUL LAMB WITH DRIED NUTS

Hussaini Korma — Kashmir

*500 g (1 lb) lamb, cut into 1 cm
  (½ in.) cubes*
salt, to taste
2 tablespoons almonds
2 tablespoons pine nuts
a little warm water
*6 tablespoons ghee or vegetable
  oil*
2 medium onions, chopped
2 tablespoons chopped ginger
1 tablespoon chopped garlic
*1 cup (250 mL, 8 fl oz) single
  (light) cream*
*1 tablespoon chopped green
  chilli peppers*
*1 tablespoon cracked white
  peppercorns*
*1 teaspoon garam masala
  (see page 134)*
*16 whole raw unsalted cashew
  nuts, shallow-fried or
  roasted (see note)*

THIS MOGUL LAMB dish reveals a Persian ancestry in its use of dried nuts. These not only impart a richness to the curry, but also act as a thickener.

Method: Place the lamb in a large bowl and rub with salt. Set aside.

Place the almonds and pine nuts in small bowl. Add just enough warm water to cover them. Set aside.

Heat 3 tablespoons of the ghee or vegetable oil in a large saucepan. Add the onion and sauté until soft and transparent. Add the ginger and garlic. Sauté for 1 minute. Remove from the heat and allow to cool. Purée in a blender or food processor.

Heat the remaining ghee in the same pan. Add the onion purée. Sauté for 2–3 minutes. Add the lamb and stir-fry for about 5 minutes, until the meat is sealed on all sides. Reduce the heat to a simmer and cover the pan with a lid. Simmer for 10–12 minutes.

Meanwhile, make a paste of the almonds and pine nuts in a blender, using as little water as possible. Add this paste to the lamb and stir thoroughly. Now add the cream, chilli peppers and white peppercorns. Simmer for further 10–12 minutes, until the lamb is cooked and the sauce is thick. Stir in the garam masala. Remove from the heat and serve immediately, garnished with the cashew nuts.

Note: The cashews can either be shallow-fried in a little oil or dry-roasted over a low heat until golden.

LAMB WITH ALMONDS
Gosht Badami Korma — Agra

1¼ cups (300 mL, 10 fl oz)
   water
500 g (1 lb) lean lamb, cut into
   1 cm (½ in.) cubes
4 cloves garlic
salt, to taste
2 tablespoons chopped
   coriander (cilantro) leaves
   (reserve the stalks and
   trimmings)
4 tablespoons ghee or vegetable
   oil
4 green (small) cardamom
   pods
5 cm (2 in.) piece of cinnamon
   stick
scant ½ cup (100 mL, 3 fl oz)
   single (light) cream
100 g (3 oz) almond paste
   (see note)
whole almonds, blanched, to
   garnish (optional)

A SIGNATURE DISH from the Moguls. Every Muslim household has its own version of this recipe. Whatever the recipe, it is always very tasty, yet still very mild. The flavour of almond and cardamom laced with cream gives the dish its exquisite taste.

Method: Combine the water, lamb, garlic, salt and any coriander trimmings in a large saucepan. Bring to a fast boil, reduce the heat and simmer for 10–12 minutes. Remove the lamb from the liquid and set aside. Strain and reserve the cooking liquid.

Heat the ghee or vegetable oil in a large clean saucepan. Add the cardamom and cinnamon. Sauté for 1 minute. Add the lamb and stir-fry for 3–4 minutes, until the lamb is sealed on the outside. Reduce the heat, then add the reserved cooking liquid and the cream. Simmer for 4–5 minutes. Stir in the almond paste and coriander leaves. Simmer for a further 5 minutes. Check the seasoning and add more salt if necessary. Remove from the heat and serve immediately, garnished with some blanched almonds (if using).

Almond paste: Do not use commercial almond paste as this contains sugar and is used for confectionery. To make your own almond paste, dry-roast ½ cup (100 g, 3 oz) of almonds in a heavy saucepan or on a roasting tray in a moderate (180°C/350°F/gas mark 4) oven for 10–15 minutes. Be careful not to scorch the almonds. Allow to cool. Roughly chop in a blender or food processor. Add just enough water to make a paste and blend until smooth. Alternatively, replace the almond paste with ¾ cup (100 g, 3 oz) of almond meal, but make sure it is not old or rancid.

LAMB IN YOGHURT WITH SPICES

Rogan Josh — Kashmir

6 whole red chilli peppers
a little warm water
3 tablespoons ghee or vegetable
  oil
3 whole cloves
3 whole cardamom pods
5 cm (2 in.) piece of cinnamon
  stick
2 bay leaves
2 medium onions, chopped
2 tablespoons chopped ginger
1 tablespoon chopped garlic
500 g (1 lb) lamb, cut into
  1 cm (1/2 in.) cubes
2 teaspoons ground turmeric
salt, to taste
2/3 cup (150 g, 5 oz) plain
  yoghurt
1 1/4 cups (300 mL, 10 fl oz)
  water
a few strands of saffron
  (optional)

PROBABLY THE MOST FAMOUS of Indian lamb curries, this classic dish has spawned numerous variations. Some argue that tomatoes are essential, while others insist on the yoghurt. A very rich dish with a good film of oil (*rogan*) on top, this modern variation calls for far less cooking fat, in keeping with contemporary dietary habits, than did its forebears.

Method: Soak the red chilli peppers in warm water for 10–15 minutes. Transfer to a blender or food processor. Blend or process into a paste. Set aside.

Heat the ghee or vegetable oil in a large saucepan over a medium-high heat. Add the cloves, cardamom, cinnamon and bay leaves. When they start to change colour, add the onion. Sauté until the onion is golden in colour. Reduce the heat to medium and add the ginger and garlic. Sauté for 4–5 minutes. Add the lamb, ground turmeric and salt. Stir-fry for 5–8 minutes, until the meat is sealed on all sides.

Whisk the yoghurt until smooth and silky. Stir into the lamb mixture. Bring to the boil, stirring continuously. Add the water and chilli paste. Reduce the heat and simmer for 15–20 minutes, until the lamb is done. Add the saffron threads (if using). Remove from the heat and serve immediately.

PORK

PORK IS COMMONLY used in regions where Chinese influence is strong. However, because of the religious beliefs of its Muslim community, pork never became widely popular in India, except in Goa, where centuries of Portuguese rule helped dispel any taboos. It is from there we inherit the world-famous hot pork curry, Pork Vindaloo.

Pork is also very popular in Bali — a stronghold of Hinduism in Indonesia — and is a must for any Hindu festival. I have devised the following recipes to embrace different styles of cooking and to show the great versatility of pork.

PORK CURRY

Wetha Hin — Burma

500 g (1 lb) lean pork, trimmed
   of any excess fat and diced
1 tablespoon ground turmeric
salt, to taste
2 tablespoons sesame oil
2 medium onions, chopped
2 tablespoons chopped ginger
1 tablespoon chopped garlic
2 tablespoons red chilli powder
2 cups (500 mL, 16 fl oz) water
1 stalk lemon grass
1 tablespoon fish sauce
2 tablespoons tamarind water
   (see glossary)
1 tablespoon chopped coriander
   (cilantro) leaves

THE COMBINATION OF onion, garlic, ginger, chilli, turmeric and sesame oil put the unmistakable stamp of Burma on this curry.

Method: Rub the pork with the ground turmeric and salt. Set aside to marinate.

Heat the sesame oil in a frying pan or skillet over a medium heat. Add the onion and sauté until soft. Reduce the heat to low. Add the ginger, garlic and chilli powder. Sauté for 2–3 minutes. Add the pork and stir-fry for about 15 minutes, until the meat is sealed on all sides. Add the water, lemon grass and fish sauce. Cook over a low heat for 8–10 minutes, until done.

Add the tamarind water and cook for a further 2–3 minutes. Garnish with the coriander leaves. Serve hot with rice.

PORK IN COCONUT MILK

Babi Lemak — Indonesia

500 g (1 lb) lean pork, diced
salt, to taste
1 cm (1/2 in.) piece of blachan
4 tablespoons sesame oil
2 medium onions, chopped
2 tablespoons chopped ginger
1 stalk lemon grass
4 whole red chilli peppers
1 1/3 cups (350 mL, 11 fl oz)
*   coconut milk*
2 teaspoons sugar
2 teaspoons brown vinegar

PORK AND COCONUT BLEND very well — a delicious combination found from Southeast Asia to the Konkan coast of India. The pork should be free of fat to bring out the delicate balance of flavours.

Method: Rub the pork with salt and set aside for 15–20 minutes.

Dry-roast the blachan in a heavy saucepan until fragrant. Transfer to a blender or food processor. Grind to a powder in a spice or coffee grinder. Set aside.

Heat the sesame oil in a large saucepan over a medium heat. Add the onion and sauté until soft. Add the ginger, blachan powder, lemon grass and chilli peppers. Sauté for 1 minute. Add the pork and stir-fry for 5–10 minutes, until the meat is sealed on all sides. Add the coconut milk and cover the pan with a lid. Simmer for 12–15 minutes, until done. Add the sugar and vinegar, and cook for a further 2–3 minutes. Serve hot with rice or noodles.

PORK CURRY WITH GINGER

Gaeng Hang Ley — Thailand

1 stalk lemon grass, chopped
1 tablespoon chopped galangal
(8 whole red chilli peppers
1 tablespoon coriander seeds
1 tablespoon blachan, dry-
roasted (see glossary)
2 tablespoons chopped garlic
2 teaspoons ground turmeric
12 white peppercorns
a little water
3 tablespoons ginger julienne
warm water, to cover
4 tablespoons vegetable oil
500 g (1 lb) pork, cut into 1 cm
(¹⁄₂ in.) cubes
1 cup (250 mL, 8 fl oz) water
(extra)
2 tablespoons soy sauce
1 tablespoon (soft) brown sugar
2 tablespoons tamarind water
(see glossary)
2 spring onions (scallions),
sliced
2 tablespoons chopped
coriander (cilantro) leaves

A TRADITIONAL AND POPULAR dish from northern Thailand, this curry uses fatty pork pieces, rather than lean meat. The ginger is added at the end of cooking to give the dish its distinctive flavour. Lean pork can be used if you prefer.

Method: Combine the lemon grass, galangal, chilli peppers, ground coriander, blachan, garlic, ground turmeric and white peppercorns in a blender or food processor. Blend to a paste using a little water. Put the paste in a bowl with the pork. Mix thoroughly and set aside for 10–15 minutes.

Place the ginger in a separate bowl. Add enough warm water to cover and set aside.

Heat the vegetable oil in a large pan over a medium heat. Add the marinated pork and cook, stirring occasionally, for 15–20 minutes. Stir in the extra water, soy sauce, brown sugar and tamarind water. Reduce the heat to low and cook for a further 15–20 minutes, until the pork is done.

Check the seasoning and add more sugar if necessary. This should be a hot sweet and sour curry. Drain the ginger julienne and stir into the curry with the spring onions. Serve immediately with boiled rice, garnished with the coriander.

PORK CUTLETS WITH GREEN PEPPERCORNS
Panri Milagu — Kerala

8 pork cutlets (rib chops),
   trimmed of excess fat
salt, to taste
4 tablespoons vegetable oil
1 medium onion, chopped
1 tablespoon chopped ginger
1 tablespoon chopped garlic
a few curry leaves
2 medium tomatoes, chopped
1 tablespoon green peppercorns
rice flour, for dusting

THE SOUTHERN COAST OF India is also known as the Pepper Coast, and its spices made it a highly prized possession of the colonial powers. Here is a recipe that was very popular with the Anglo-Indian settlers in the spice plantations.

Method: Flatten the pork cutlets with a meat pounder. Rub with salt and set aside.

Heat 2 tablespoons of the vegetable oil in a frying pan or skillet over a medium heat. Add the onion and sauté until soft. Add the ginger, garlic and curry leaves. Sauté for 1–2 minutes. Add the tomatoes and cook over a low heat until soft. Add the peppercorns and keep warm.

Heat the remaining oil in a separate pan over a medium heat. Dust the cutlets with the rice flour. Pan-fry the cutlets for 4–5 minutes on each side, so that they cook evenly. Spoon some of the tomato mixture onto each of 4 serving plates. Add two cutlets to each plate and serve immediately, accompanied by a salad.

PORK KEBABS

Espetada — Goa

*500 g (1 lb) lean pork , cut into
1 cm (½ in.) cubes*
salt, to taste
6 dried red chilli peppers
1 tablespoon black peppercorns
6 whole cloves
*5 cm (2 in.) piece of cinnamon
stick*
2 teaspoons coriander seeds
3 tablespoons white vinegar
1 tablespoon chopped garlic
2 teaspoons ground turmeric
1 tablespoon chopped ginger
*2 tablespoons coriander
(cilantro) leaves*
a little water
*bamboo skewers, soaked in
water to prevent scorching*

A VERY POPULAR dish from Goa on the western coast of India. Goa not only has some of the best beaches in the world, but also a unique cuisine, formed by the fusion of the indigenous and Portuguese cultures.

Method: Place the pork in a bowl. Rub with salt and set aside.

Dry-roast the chilli peppers, black peppercorns, cloves, cinnamon and coriander seeds in a heavy saucepan until fragrant. Grind to a powder in a spice or coffee grinder. Transfer to a blender or food processor. Add the vinegar, garlic, ground turmeric, ginger and coriander leaves. Blend to a paste using a little water. Mix with the pork and leave to marinate for about 2 hours.

Thread the meat onto bamboo skewers and cook under a medium-hot grill (broiler). Turn the skewers frequently until the meat is cooked on all sides, about 4–5 minutes per side. (Alternatively, the pork can be char-grilled on a barbecue or pan-fried in a little vegetable oil.) Serve immediately with a spicy chutney.

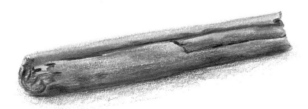

PAN-FRIED PORK CUTLETS

Wetha Katlet — Burma

4 pork cutlets (rib chops),
    trimmed of any fat
1 tablespoon chopped garlic
salt, to taste
3 tablespoons soy sauce
2 teaspoons freshly ground
    black pepper
4 whole eggs, beaten
1 cup (125 g, 4 oz) rice flour
4 tablespoons vegetable oil

ANOTHER ANGLICISED RECIPE from the Rangoon Club. Served with a dry vegetable dish and a small portion of rice, it makes a perfect dinner.

Method: Flatten the pork cutlets with a meat pounder. Combine the garlic, salt, soy sauce and black pepper in a bowl. Place the cutlets in the marinade and set aside for 10–15 minutes.

Heat the vegetable oil in a heavy frying pan or skillet over a medium heat. Dip the cutlets in the egg yolk and dredge with the rice flour. Place the cutlets in the pan and fry on both sides until golden brown. Serve with roast potatoes.

SPARE RIBS WITH SOY AND GINGER
Singapore

1 tablespoon minced garlic
1 tablespoon minced ginger
1 tablespoon cracked black
    peppercorns
2 tablespoons honey
6 tablespoons soy sauce
2 tablespoons sesame oil
salt, to taste
2 tablespoons red chilli powder
2 tablespoons garam masala
    (see page 134)
1 cup (250 mL, 8 fl oz) tomato
    sauce (ketchup)
1 kg (2 lb) pork spare ribs
a few coriander (cilantro)
    sprigs

A FUSION OF Chinese and Indian cuisines, this dish is very easy to make, yet the taste and flavours are exquisite. This recipe is 20 years old and comes from the very first restaurant in which I worked.

Method: Combine the garlic, ginger, black peppercorns, honey, soy sauce, sesame oil, salt, chilli powder, garam masala and tomato sauce in a bowl. Whisk thoroughly. Add the spare ribs, making sure that they are well coated with the marinade. Leave to marinate for at least 2-3 hours.

Preheat the oven to 200°–230°C (400°–450°F / gas mark 6–8). Place the spare ribs in a roasting pan. Cook the ribs in the oven for 15–20 minutes, basting frequently with the marinade. When done, the ribs should be a dark reddish colour. Serve hot, garnished with the coriander sprigs.

BEEF

BEEF IS ONE of those meats that adapts well to most styles of cooking. However, the very high cost of Western cuts limits their use throughout Asia and Southeast Asia, where their place is often taken by water-buffalo meat. These beasts are not reared for the table, but are usually slaughtered at the end of a hard working life. As a result, the meat tends to be fairly tough, though full of flavour, and requires long cooking times to become tender.

Western-style beef, on the other hand, is relatively tender and takes much less time to cook. It is important to simmer beef over a low heat for no longer than the specified time, in order to prevent drying out. Beef blends very well with spices, and dishes such as Beef Rendang from Indonesia, Beef Masaman from Thailand and Beef with Apricots from India have become world famous.

COCONUT BEEF CURRY

Ametha Ono Hin — Burma

500 g (1 lb) lean beef, cut into
    1 cm (½ in.) cubes
salt, to taste
1 tablespoon ground turmeric
2 tablespoons red chilli powder
    (optional)
4 tablespoons sesame oil
2 medium onions, chopped
2 tablespoons chopped ginger
1 tablespoon chopped garlic
1 stalk lemon grass, bruised
1 cup (250 mL, 8 fl oz) water
scant 1 cup (25 mL, 7 fl oz)
    coconut milk
2 tablespoons chopped
    coriander (cilantro) leaves

THIS HOME-STYLE BEEF curry is cooked when someone important is visiting or for some other auspicious occasion. The chilli powder is optional, and can be reduced or increased to suit individual taste.

Method: Place the beef in a bowl. Add the salt, ground turmeric and chilli powder (if using). Mix thoroughly. Set aside to marinate while you prepare the other ingredients.

    Heat the oil in a saucepan over a medium heat. Add the onion and sauté until soft. Add the ginger, garlic and lemon grass. Sauté for 2–3 minutes, then add the marinated beef. Cook, stirring, until the meat is sealed on all sides. Add the water and coconut milk. Bring to a fast boil, then reduce the heat and simmer for 10–15 minutes, until the meat is cooked. Remove the lemon grass. Stir through the coriander leaves and serve immediately, accompanied by boiled rice.

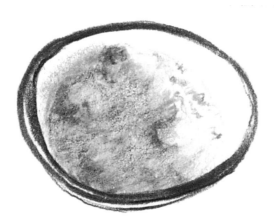

BEEF WITH POTATOES IN MUSLIM CURRY
Gaeng Masaman — Thailand

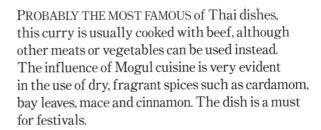

4 tablespoons coconut cream

2½ cups (625 mL, 1 imp. pint)
coconut milk

3 bay leaves

2 teaspoons whole black
peppercorns

2 cm (1 in.) piece of cinnamon
stick

4 whole cardamom pods

salt, to taste

375 g (¾ lb) stewing beef, cut
into 2 cm (1 in.) cubes

6 tablespoons muslim curry
paste (see page 132)

4 small potatoes, quartered
and deep-fried

2 tablespoons roasted peanuts

2 tablespoons fish sauce

1 tablespoon palm or brown
sugar

2 tablespoons tamarind water
(see glossary)

2 medium onions, cut into
wedges

PROBABLY THE MOST FAMOUS of Thai dishes,
this curry is usually cooked with beef, although
other meats or vegetables can be used instead.
The influence of Mogul cuisine is very evident
in the use of dry, fragrant spices such as cardamom,
bay leaves, mace and cinnamon. The dish is a must
for festivals.

Method: Combine 2 tablespoons of the coconut cream,
the coconut milk, bay leaves, black peppercorns,
cinnamon, cardamom and salt in a large saucepan.
Bring to the boil. Reduce the heat to a simmer and
add the beef. Cook for 15–20 minutes, until the beef
is tender.

Meanwhile, heat the remaining coconut cream in
a medium saucepan over a medium heat. When the
oil starts to separate from the cream, add the curry
paste. Cook, stirring continuously, for 2–3 minutes.
Add the potatoes and peanuts. Cook, still stirring,
for 1–2 minutes, or until the potatoes and peanuts
are well coated with the paste. Add the beef and its
cooking liquid, the fish sauce, palm or brown sugar,
tamarind water and onion. Simmer over a medium
heat for 8–10 minutes, or until the beef is tender.

Check the seasoning; the dish should be sweet
and tangy. Add a little fish sauce, sugar or tamarind
water if necessary. Serve hot.

BEEF WITH APRICOTS

Sali Boti — India

8 dried apricots
water, to cover
4 tablespoons vegetable oil
5 cm (2 in.) piece of cinnamon
  stick
4 whole cloves
3 small whole cardamom pods
2 medium onions, chopped
2 tablespoons chopped ginger
1 tablespoon chopped garlic
2 teaspoons red chilli powder
1½ teaspoons ground turmeric
1½ tablespoons ground cumin
2 teaspoons ground coriander
2 medium tomatoes, chopped
500 g (1 lb) lean beef, cut into
  1 cm (½ in.) cubes
salt, to taste
2 tablespoons vinegar or
  tamarind water
  (see glossary)
1 tablespoon palm or brown
  sugar
2 tablespoons chopped
  coriander (cilantro) leaves
60 g (2 oz) potato straws
  (shoestring potatoes)
  (see note)

A DISH FROM the Parsee community in India. The Parsees fled Persia about 2000 years ago to escape religious persecution. Their cuisine is a unique blend of Gujerati and Persian influences, evidenced by the extensive use of dried fruits and the balance of sweet and sour tastes in their dishes.

Method: Place the apricots in a bowl. Add just enough water to cover. Set aside at room temperature.

Heat the vegetable oil in a saucepan over a medium heat. Add the cinnamon, cloves and cardamom. Sauté for 1 minute. Add the onion and sauté until the onion is golden brown. Reduce the heat and add the ginger and garlic. Sauté for 1–2 minutes. Add the chilli powder, ground turmeric, ground cumin and ground coriander. Sauté for 1 minute before adding the tomatoes. Cook, stirring, for 4–5 minutes. Add the beef and salt. Cook, stirring continuously, for 5–10 minutes.

Cover the pan with a lid and simmer for 15–20 minutes, until the beef is nearly done. Drain the apricots of any excess water and add to the meat with the vinegar or tamarind water. Stir through, then add the sugar. Simmer for 3–4 minutes. Check the seasoning and add salt if necessary. Stir in the coriander leaves. Serve immediately, garnished with the potato straws.

Potato straws: These can be bought in packets from the supermarket. However, if you prefer to make your own, peel and cut 2 medium potatoes into matchstick-size julienne. Pat dry and deep-fry until golden brown and crisp. Drain on paper towels (absorbent kitchen paper).

BEEF BAFFAT

Bada Gosht Baffat — Bombay

6 whole red chilli peppers

2 tablespoons chopped ginger

2 tablespoons chopped garlic

1 tablespoon cumin seeds

4 whole cloves

5 cm (2 in.) piece of cinnamon
stick

2 teaspoons ground turmeric

2 tablespoons white vinegar

4 tablespoons ghee or
vegetable oil

3 medium onions, chopped

375 g (³/4 lb) lean beef, cut into
1 cm (¹/2 in.) cubes

salt, to taste

2 medium tomatoes, chopped

125 g (¹/4 lb) small potatoes,
peeled

4 tablespoons tamarind water
(see glossary)

1 tablespoon palm or brown
sugar

COMBINING DRIED FRUITS, with their sweet and sour flavours, makes Parsee cuisine different from that of the rest of India. Chicken or lamb can be substituted for the beef if desired.

*Method:*Combine the chilli peppers, ginger, garlic, cumin seeds, cloves, cinnamon, ground turmeric and vinegar in a blender or food processor. Blend to a fine paste (a little water can be added if necessary).

Heat the ghee or vegetable oil in a large saucepan over a medium heat. Add the onion and sauté until golden brown. Add the paste. Sauté for 2–3 minutes before adding the beef and salt. Cover the pan with a lid and cook, stirring occasionally, for 10–12 minutes (add a little water if the mixture becomes too dry). Add the tomatoes and potatoes. Reduce the heat to low and cook for 10–15 minutes, until the potatoes are nearly done. Stir in the tamarind water and sugar. Check the seasoning and adjust with a little sugar or tamarind if necessary.

Remove from the heat and allow to cool for 30–40 minutes — this allows the flavours to blend. Reheat gently just before serving.

BEEF HOT POT

Kerala Istew — India

4 tablespoons vegetable oil
2 bay leaves
4 whole red chilli peppers
2 teaspoons brown mustard
  seeds
6 black peppercorns
1 medium onion, chopped
1 tablespoon chopped ginger
1 tablespoon chopped garlic
500 g (1 lb) lean beef, cut into 1
  cm (½ in.) cubes
salt, to taste
1 tablespoon rice flour
2 teaspoons ground turmeric
1²/₃ cups (400 mL, 13 fl oz)
  coconut milk
1 tablespoon chopped green
  chilli peppers
2 medium potatoes, peeled and
  cut into 1 cm (½ in.) cubes
½ cup (100 g, 3 oz) green
  (French, string) beans, diced
2 medium carrots, diced
a few curry leaves
2 tablespoons tamarind water
  (see glossary)

THE BACKWATERS OF KERALA probably constitute the most beautiful region of southern India. Idyllic palm groves, plentiful food and an easygoing lifestyle have made it greatly envied. The population is an equal balance of Hindu, Muslim and Christian, and Keralan cuisine reflects generous borrowings from each of these cultures over the ages. This recipe is from the Syrian Christian community.

Method: Heat 3 tablespoons of the vegetable oil in a large saucepan over a medium heat. Add the bay leaves, red chilli peppers, mustard seeds, black peppercorns and onion. Sauté until the onion is transparent. Add the ginger and garlic. Sauté for 1–2 minutes. Add the beef and salt. Cook, stirring, until the meat is sealed on all sides. Add the rice flour and ground turmeric. Cook, still stirring, for 1–2 minutes. Add 1¼ cups (300 mL, 10 fl oz) of the coconut milk and the green chilli peppers. Reduce the heat to low and cook for 15–20 minutes, until the beef is almost done.

Meanwhile, sauté the vegetables in the remaining oil and add to the stew. Cook for a further 10–15 minutes, until the vegetables are done. Add the remaining coconut milk, curry leaves and tamarind water. Check the seasoning and adjust with salt if necessary. Remove from the heat and let stand for 20–25 minutes to allow the flavours to blend. Reheat gently just before serving.

BEEF RENDANG

Rendang Padang — Indonesia

2 medium onions, chopped
2 teaspoons chopped garlic
1 tablespoon chopped ginger
2 tablespoons red chilli powder
1 tablespoon ground turmeric
1 tablespoon ground coriander
2½ cups (625 mL, 1 imp. pint)
    coconut milk
2 tablespoons vegetable oil
3 whole cloves
5 cm (2 in.) piece of cinnamon
    stick
650 g (1¼ lb) lean beef, cut into
    2 cm (1 in.) cubes
salt, to taste
2 tablespoons tamarind water
    (see glossary)
1 tablespoon brown sugar

A VERY FAMOUS beef dish from Sumatra. The finished meal is dark red in colour, with a rich and spicy flavour imparted by the blend of coconut milk and spices. It is usually served with rice and a side dish or two of vegetables.

Method: Combine the onion, garlic, ginger, red chilli powder, ground turmeric and ground coriander in a blender or food processor. Add a little of the coconut milk and blend to a paste (use as little coconut milk as possible).

Heat the vegetable oil in a large saucepan over a medium heat. Add the cloves and cinnamon. Reduce the heat and add the paste. Sauté for 1–2 minutes, then add the beef and salt. Cook, stirring, until the meat is sealed on all sides. Add the coconut milk and bring to the boil. Reduce the heat to low and simmer for 20–25 minutes, until the beef is tender. Add the tamarind water and sugar. Check the seasoning and adjust with a little tamarind or sugar if necessary. Serve immediately.

KADAI-COOKED BEEF

Kadai Bada Gosht — India

500 g (1 lb) lean beef, cut into
    1 cm (½ in.) cubes
2 bay leaves
2 small whole cardamom pods
2 whole cloves
salt, to taste
a little water
4 tablespoons vegetable oil
3 medium onions, chopped
2 tablespoons chopped ginger
1 tablespoon chopped garlic
2 medium tomatoes, chopped
1 tablespoon crushed coriander
    seeds
1 tablespoon crushed dried red
    chilli peppers
4 chopped green chilli peppers
2 tablespoons chopped
    coriander (cilantro) leaves
1 teaspoon garam masala
    (see page 134)

KADAI (WOK) COOKING is very popular in northwest India. Unlike in China, the main ingredients are not added raw, but are partially cooked and then mixed with fresh herbs, spices and vegetables to give a distinctive taste and appearance. It is a cuisine that is best cooked at the last moment, as it loses its unique flavours if reheated. You should first assemble all the ingredients on a tray and start to cook just before serving.

Method: Combine the beef with the bay leaves, cardamom, cloves and salt. Place in a saucepan and add enough water to cover. Simmer over a medium heat for 10–12 minutes, until half cooked. Set aside.

Heat the vegetable oil in a *kadai* or heavy wok. Add the onion and stir-fry until transparent. Add 1 tablespoon of the ginger and the garlic. Stir-fry for 1–2 minutes, then add the tomatoes. Cook over a high heat until the tomatoes are pulpy, but not thoroughly cooked.

Add the beef, without its juices, and stir-fry for 5–7 minutes, until nearly done. Check the seasoning and adjust with salt if necessary. Add the coriander seeds and red chilli peppers. Stir-fry for 1–2 minutes. Add the remaining ginger, green chilli peppers, coriander leaves and garam masala. Serve immediately.

Sour Beef Stew

Samlor Mochu — Cambodia

2 tablespoons chopped garlic
6 Kaffir lime leaves
1 tablespoon galangal
1 tablespoon ground turmeric
1 stalk lemon grass
1 tablespoon red chilli powder
a little water
4 tablespoons vegetable oil
500 g (1 lb) lean beef, diced
scant 1 cup (225 mL, 7 fl oz)
   water
2 tablespoons fish sauce
2 tablespoons tamarind water
   (see glossary)
2 tablespoons sliced spring
   onions (scallions)

A BEEF DISH FROM the kingdom of Cambodia. Unlike other cuisines of the Southeast Asian region, Cambodian cuisine does not use sugar to counter the tartness of tamarind.

Method: Combine the garlic, lime leaves, galangal, ground turmeric, lemon grass and chilli powder in a blender or food processor. Add a little water and blend to a paste (use as little water as possible).

Heat the vegetable oil in a large saucepan over a medium heat. Add the paste and sauté for 1–2 minutes. Add the beef and sauté for 2–3 minutes, then add the water and fish sauce. Bring to a fast boil, then reduce the heat to a simmer. Cook the beef for 20–25 minutes, until nearly done. Add the tamarind water and simmer for 2–3 minutes. Check the seasoning and add more tamarind if necessary. Serve immediately, garnished with the spring onion.

VEGETABLES & LEGUMES

I THINK IT IS VERY difficult to find a 'genuine' vegetarian meal anywhere outside India. There, 50 to 60 per cent of the population are strict vegetarians, and no meal is complete without a legume in some form or other, from a simple *papad* to an exotic dhal. In other parts of Asia, vegetarian meals often contain one or more non-vegetarian ingredients, such as shrimp, blachan or fish sauce.

Most of the recipes in this chapter come from India, the home of vegetarian cuisine, but I have used a variety of ingredients and cooking methods to illustrate the astonishing versatility of simple legumes and vegetables.

MIXED VEGETABLE CURRY

Hintiyeet Hintamyo — Burma

4 tablespoons sesame oil
2 medium onions, chopped
2 tablespoons chopped ginger
1 tablespoon chopped garlic
1 tablespoon ground turmeric
a small piece of blachan
2 tablespoons shrimp powder
500 g (1 lb) mixed vegetables,
*   cut into 1 cm (¹/₂ in.) cubes*
4 green chilli peppers, chopped
1¹/₄ cups (300 mL, 10 fl oz)
*   coconut milk*
a little water
salt, to taste
2 tablespoons coriander
*   (cilantro) leaves, chopped*

BURMA IS A VERY FERTILE land, where vegetables grow all year round. Fresh produce is always used in Burmese cooking; cans and frozen foods are unheard of. Use seasonal vegetables to get the best results from this recipe.

Method: Heat the oil in a large saucepan. Add the onion and sauté until soft. Add the ginger, garlic, turmeric, blachan and shrimp powder. Sauté for 2-3 minutes. Add the vegetables and green chilli peppers, and cook over a medium heat for 5-7 minutes, until tender. Now add the coconut milk and a little water if the sauce is too thick. Check the seasoning and adjust with salt if necessary. Serve hot, garnished with the coriander leaves.

BANANA CHILLI CURRY
Hyderabadi Chilli Koora — India

16 banana chilli peppers
3 tablespoons peeled raw
    peanuts
1/2 tablespoon sesame seeds
1/2 tablespoon cumin seeds
1 tablespoon coriander seeds
5 tablespoons vegetable oil
2 medium onions, chopped
1 tablespoon chopped ginger
1 tablespoon chopped garlic
1/2 tablespoon tamarind pulp,
    dissolved in 2 tablespoons
    water
salt, to taste

THIS FAIRLY DRY DISH originates from the princely
state of Hyderabad. The house of Nizam was famous
not only for its wealth, but also for its banquets.
This is not a spicy dish; the banana chilli peppers are
used more for their flavour than their bite. Many
chefs add hot chilli powder to make the dish spicy,
but I prefer the original version.

Method: Cut the banana chilli peppers into slices
or discs. Dry-roast the peanuts and the sesame, cumin
and coriander seeds. Transfer to a blender or food
processor and grind to a coarse powder. Heat the oil in
a large saucepan and sauté the banana chilli peppers
for 3–5 minutes. Remove from the pan and set aside.
In the same pan, sauté the onion until light brown.
Add the ginger and garlic and sauté for 2–3 minutes.
Now add the powder mixture and fry for a further
2–3 minutes. Add the banana chilli peppers and the
tamarind pulp and stir-fry for 3–5 minutes. Check the
seasoning and adjust with salt if necessary. Serve hot.

SPICED CHICKPEAS WITH TOMATOES AND CORIANDER

Channa Masala — Punjab

450 g (14 oz) canned chickpeas
4 tablespoons vegetable oil
2 bay leaves
½ tablespoon cumin seeds
1 tablespoon chopped ginger
1 tablespoon chopped chilli
*   peppers*
½ tablespoon ground cumin
½ tablespoon ground coriander
½ tablespoon red chilli powder
¼ tablespoon ground turmeric
½ tablespoon dried mango
*   powder* (amchur*) or lemon*
*   juice*
salt, to taste
2 medium tomatoes, quartered
2 tablespoons coriander
*   (cilantro) leaves, chopped*

PULSES FORM a very important part of Indian, especially Punjabi, cuisine. Channas or chickpeas are the most popular of all. There are many ways of cooking channas, but this is my favourite. I have used canned chickpeas here, but you can also use the dry variety — just soak them overnight with a pinch of salt, and cook over a low heat for 1 hour or in a pressure-cooker for 20–25 minutes.

Method: Drain and wash the chickpeas. Set aside. Heat the oil in a large saucepan. Add the bay leaves and cumin seeds and stir-fry for 1–2 minutes. Reduce the heat. Add the ginger and the chilli peppers and stir-fry for 2–3 minutes. Now add the ground cumin, coriander, chilli powder and the turmeric. Stir-fry over a low heat until dark brown, but not burnt.

Add the chickpeas and simmer for 10–15 minutes, until the mixture coats the chickpeas. Add the mango powder or lemon juice. Check the seasoning and adjust with salt if necessary. Garnish with the tomatoes and coriander and serve with a crusty bread.

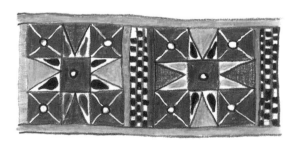

MUSHROOMS WITH DRIED FRUITS AND POPPY SEEDS

Khumbi Rizala — North-West Frontier, Pakistan

60 g (2 oz) poppy seeds
100 g (3 oz) whole almonds
a little water
4 tablespoons ghee or
*   vegetable oil*
3 bay leaves
1/3 tablespoon onion seeds
*   (nigela)*
1/3 tablespoon cumin seeds
2 medium onions, puréed
2 tablespoons chopped ginger
1 tablespoon chopped garlic
4 green chilli peppers, chopped
1/2 cup (125 g, 4 oz) yoghurt,
*   whisked*
salt, to taste
450 g (14 oz) button
*   mushrooms*
150 g (5 oz) uncooked green
*   peas*
1/2 tablespoon coriander seeds
2 tablespoons coriander
*   (cilantro) leaves, chopped*

THIS IS A VEGETARIAN adaptation of a famous meat dish. The use of dried fruits and poppy seeds is very typical of the region, where both grow in abundance. The dried fruits not only impart a nutty and rich flavour, but also act as a thickener.

Method: Combine the poppy seeds and almonds. Dry-roast in a frying pan or skillet over a medium heat for about 3 minutes. Set aside to cool. Transfer to a blender or food processor and blend with enough water to make a thick paste.

Heat 3 tablespoons of the ghee or vegetable oil in a large saucepan. Add the bay leaves and onion and cumin seeds. Reduce the heat, add the puréed onion and sauté over a medium heat for 4–5 minutes. Now add the ginger, garlic and chilli peppers and sauté for 2–3 minutes. Add the yoghurt and stir until the mixture starts to boil. Reduce the heat and leave to simmer for 4–5 minutes. Add the salt.

In a large saucepan, heat the remaining ghee or vegetable oil and sauté the mushrooms and green peas for 3–4 minutes. Add to the sauce, mix in the almond and poppy-seed paste and simmer for 4–5 minutes. Finish off by stirring in the coriander seeds and leaves.

CAULIFLOWER WITH FENNEL AND GINGER
Gobi Kashmiri — Kashmir

4 tablespoons ghee or vegetable
   oil
450 g (14 oz) cauliflower
   florets
2 medium onions, chopped
2 tablespoons chopped ginger
1 tablespoon ground coriander
1½ tablespoons red chilli
   powder
3 medium tomatoes, chopped
½ tablespoon fennel seeds
½ tablespoon ground ginger
¼ tablespoon small (green)
   cardamom pods, ground to
   a powder
salt, to taste
2 tablespoons coriander
   (cilantro) leaves, chopped

A VERY TASTY DISH from Kashmir, a region famed for its picturesque valleys and mountains, and also known as the Switzerland of the East. Kashmiri cuisine is very distinct from north Indian, with an emphasis on the use of ginger and fennel.

Method: Heat 2 tablespoons of the ghee or vegetable oil in a large frying pan or skillet. Add the cauliflower florets and sauté over a medium heat for 5–7 minutes. Set aside. In the same pan, heat the remaining ghee or vegetable oil and sauté the onion over a medium heat until brown. Add the chopped ginger, ground coriander, chilli powder and tomatoes. Sauté for 4–5 minutes. Add the cauliflower and cook covered for 4–5 minutes until nearly done. Remove the lid and stir in the ground fennel, ginger and cardamom, taking care not to break the cauliflower florets. Leave on the heat for a further 2 minutes. Check the seasoning and adjust with salt if necessary. Add the coriander leaves just before serving.

Fennel/cardamom powder: Dry-roast the seeds/pods over a low heat. Allow to cool, then grind to a powder in a spice or coffee grinder.

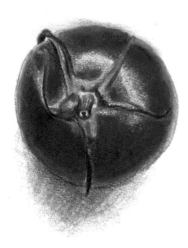

CHICKPEAS WITH GINGER
Chole Adraki — Punjab

450 g (14 oz) canned chickpeas
4 tablespoons ghee or vegetable
 oil
3 medium onions, chopped
1 tablespoon chopped garlic
3 tablespoons chopped ginger
½ tablespoon cumin seeds
1 tablespoon coriander seeds,
 crushed
3 medium tomatoes, chopped
salt, to taste
4 green chilli peppers, chopped
1 tablespoon dried red chilli
 peppers, crushed
lemon juice, to taste
1 tablespoon fenugreek leaves

CHICKPEAS ARE AS POPULAR in north and central
India as they are throughout the Middle East.
They are very nutritious and still form an integral
part of the diet of athletes and body builders. I have
used canned chickpeas here, but you can also use the
dry variety — just soak them overnight with a pinch
of salt, and cook over low a heat for 1 hour or in a
pressure-cooker for 20–25 minutes.

Method: Drain the chickpeas and set aside. Heat the
ghee or vegetable oil in a large saucepan. Add the
onion and sauté over a medium heat until soft. Add
the garlic and ½ tablespoon of the ginger. Sauté for
1–2 minutes, then add the cumin and coriander seeds
and tomatoes. Cook over a medium heat 7–10 minutes,
until the sauce thickens. Now add the chickpeas, salt,
green and red chilli peppers. Cook for 10–12 minutes
or until the chickpeas are coated with the sauce.
Finish off by adding the lemon juice, remaining
ginger and fenugreek leaves. Check the seasoning
and adjust with salt if necessary. Serve hot.

EGGPLANT WITH LENTILS AND SPICES

Baingan Bagar — Maharashtra

4 tablespoons ghee or
    vegetable oil
1 medium onion, sliced
4 tablespoons desiccated
    (shredded) coconut
6 whole red chilli peppers
1 tablespoon coriander seeds
5 cm (2 in.) cinnamon stick
½ tablespoon chopped garlic
2 tablespoons channa dhal
a few curry leaves
12 small eggplants
    (aubergines)
1–2 teaspoons ghee or
    vegetable oil
salt, to taste
1 tablespoon coriander
    (cilantro) leaves, chopped

FROM THE WESTERN GHATS mountain range in southern India, this recipe uses lentils and spices to give this dish its unique roasted, earthy flavours.

Method: Heat 4 tablespoons of the ghee or vegetable oil in a large frying pan (skillet). Add the onion and cook over a medium heat until golden brown. Add the coconut, chilli peppers, coriander seeds, cinnamon stick, garlic, channa dhal and curry leaves. Fry over a low heat for 4–5 minutes, until a pleasant aroma rises from the pan. Remove and cool to room temperature. Transfer to a blender or food processor and blend to a coarse paste.

Slit the eggplants into four from bottom to top, leaving them joined at the top end. Stuff with the paste. Tie the quarters loosely together with cotton string.

Heat 1 or 2 teaspoons of ghee or vegetable oil in a large frying pan (skillet). Fry the eggplants over a medium heat for 8–10 minutes, turning frequently to ensure even cooking. Alternatively, grill (broil) them under a griller (broiler). Check the seasoning and adjust with salt if necessary. Serve hot, garnished with the chopped coriander.

SPICED SMALL POTATOES

Hyderabadi Chats — India

350 g (11 oz) small new
    potatoes (chats)
salt, to taste
3 tablespoons ghee or vegetable
    oil
1 tablespoon cumin seeds
½ tablespoon asafoetida powder
½ tablespoon ground turmeric
½ tablespoon dried mango
    powder (amchur)
3 tablespoons fresh mint,
    chopped
2 tablespoons chopped ginger
1 tablespoon chopped chilli
    peppers

A SIMPLE YET DELICIOUS dish from the Deccan region of India, where Muslim and south Indian cuisines combine, it is usually served to accompany lamb.

Method: Boil the potatoes in salted water for 15–20 minutes, until nearly done. Remove from the water and allow to cool. Peel and set aside.

Heat the ghee or vegetable oil in a wok. Add the cumin and asafoetida. Reduce the heat to low, and add the turmeric, dried mango powder and potatoes. Sauté for 5–6 minutes over a low heat, until the potatoes are coated with the paste. Add the mint, ginger and chilli peppers. Toss for 1–2 minutes. Serve hot.

VEGETABLE ROLLS
Sabzi — Punjab

2 tablespoons vegetable oil
½ tablespoon cumin seeds
pinch of asafoetida powder
1 tablespoon chopped ginger
1 tablespoon green chilli
    peppers, chopped
⅓ tablespoon ground turmeric
½ tablespoon red chilli powder
185 g (6 oz) boiled potatoes, cut
    into 1 cm (½ in.) cubes
salt, to taste
100 g (3 oz) uncooked peas
¼ tablespoon dried mango
    powder (amchur)
1 tablespoon coriander
    (cilantro) leaves, chopped
12 pastry sheets (spring-roll
    skins)
egg, channa besan or plain
    (all-purpose) flour, for
    sealing
vegetable oil, for frying

A HEARTY SNACK from the Punjab, sabzi are ancient India's contribution to fast food. They can be served as a breakfast, lunch or evening snack, and with a cup of tea (*chai*) form a perfect light meal. Traditionally made with potatoes and peas, they also appear in meaty variations. For these rolls, I have substituted pastry sheets instead of short-crust dough. I find it lighter and much faster to prepare.

Method: Heat the oil in a wok. Add the cumin seeds, reduce the heat and add the asafoetida, ginger, chilli peppers, ground turmeric and chilli powder. Sauté for 1 minute. Now add the potatoes and fry for 2–3 minutes. Add the salt, green peas, mango powder and coriander leaves. Sauté for 2–3 minutes. Remove from the wok and allow to cool.

Lay out the pastry sheets, and place a tablespoon or two of the stuffing in one corner of each. Roll up each sheet, fold in the sides and seal the ends with egg or flour.

Deep-fry the rolls in medium–hot oil until golden brown. Serve the rolls with a tomato salsa.

RICE AND NOODLES

RICE OR NOODLES form the staple foods of Asia, with noodles becoming popular in regions under Chinese influence, and other areas remaining basically rice eating.

Noodles generally occur in combination dishes, with vegetables and/or meat, and are often a one-dish meal. When cooking noodles, it is important to follow the instructions carefully.

Rice is cultivated in many varieties and in many countries of tropical and sub-tropical Asia. Indian cuisine probably includes the broadest repertoire of rice cookery, with Basmati rice the best for pulaos and biryanis. However, any long-grain variety will yield satisfying results.

Generally speaking, the following dishes use rice as the main component and the curry as a moistener.

CUMIN RICE

Jeera Pulao — India

3 tablespoons vegetable oil
2 bay leaves
½ tablespoon cumin seeds
2 medium onions, chopped
1¾ cups long-grain or Basmati rice
2¾ cups (700 mL, 22 fl oz) water

THIS RICE DISH can be served with all kinds of Indian curries. It is best made immediately before serving.

Method: Heat the oil in a large pan. Add the bay leaves and cumin seeds. Fry for 1-2 minutes. Add the onion and sauté until transparent. Add the rice and fry until well coated, then add the water and cook, stirring occasionally, for 10-15 minutes, until done.

COCONUT RICE

Khao Man — Thailand

2 cups Jasmine rice
2 cups (500 mL, 16 fl oz) water
2 cups (500 mL, 16 fl oz)
coconut milk
salt, to taste
½ tablespoon sugar

RICE IN SOME FORM or other always forms a significant part of a Southeast Asian meal. Not only is it very versatile, but it is also a good filler. Here, coconut supplements the cooking water.

Method: Wash the rice in cold water, then set aside to drain. In a large pan, combine the rice, water, coconut milk, salt and sugar. Bring to a fast boil, stirring occasionally. Reduce the heat and cover. Cook for 15–18 minutes, until done. Remove from the heat, take off the lid and fluff the rice with a roasting fork, taking care not to mash the grains. Serve hot.

COCONUT AND SESAME RICE
Ellu Sadam — Kerala

3 tablespoons vegetable oil
a pinch of asafoetida powder
½ tablespoon mustard seeds
½ tablespoon urad dhal
   (see glossary)
a few curry leaves
3 tablespoons desiccated
   (shredded) coconut
½ tablespoon sesame seeds
3 cups cold cooked rice (keep in
   refrigerator overnight)
salt, to taste

ANOTHER FAVOURITE from the south of India.

Method: Heat the oil in a large frying pan (skillet). Add the asafeotida and mustard seeds. When the seeds start to sputter, add the urad dhal and reduce the heat. After 1 minute, add the curry leaves, coconut and sesame seeds. Brown on a low heat so as not to burn.

Put the rice in a mixing bowl and combine with the fried mixture. Check the seasoning, adding salt if required. Serve at room temperature or reheated, as desired.

LEMON RICE

Nimbu Chawal — Madras

6 tablespoons vegetable oil
4 tablespoons peanuts
a pinch of asafoetida powder
½ tablespoon mustard seeds
½ tablespoon channa dhal
   (see glossary)
½ tablespoon ground turmeric
½ tablespoon chopped ginger
½ tablespoon green chilli
   peppers, chopped
a few curry leaves
3 cups cold boiled rice
juice of two lemons
salt, to taste
4 tablespoons desiccated
   (shredded) coconut,
   dry-roasted

AN ALL-TIME FAVOURITE from the south coast of India, this dish is usually made with leftover rice. It is served at room temperature rather than hot, though it may be heated just before serving. The rice can be cooked the previous day and kept in the refrigerator.

Method: Heat the oil in a large frying pan (skillet). Fry the peanuts over medium heat until lightly browned. Remove and set aside. To the same pan add the asafoetida and mustard seeds and return to the heat. When the seeds begin to sputter, add the channa dhal and stir-fry for 2–3 minutes. Reduce the heat and add the turmeric, ginger, chilli peppers and curry leaves.

Place the rice in a bowl and add the fried mixture. Add the lemon juice, and salt, if necessary. Mix well and serve at room temperature or hot, garnished with the coconut.

YELLOW RICE

Nasi Kuning — Indonesia

4 tablespoons vegetable or
   peanut oil
1 large onion, chopped
1 tablespoon chopped garlic
1 stalk lemon grass, sliced
1⅓ cups long-grain rice
½ tablespoon ground turmeric
1 cup (250 mL, 8 fl oz) coconut
   milk
¾ cup (185 mL, 6 fl oz) water

THE YELLOW COLOUR OF THIS excellent rice dish from Indonesia is imparted by the ground turmeric during cooking. The blend of coconut milk and rice provides its unique flavour and taste. It is usually served with lots of accompaniments, the most common being chunks of cucumber, omelette strips and peanut sauce.

Method: Heat the oil in a medium saucepan. Add the onion and sauté until transparent. Add the garlic and lemon grass, fry for 1 minute, then add the rice and turmeric. Stir-fry carefully until all the rice grains are evenly coated with a film of oil. Add the coconut milk and water. Stir well and bring to a boil. Reduce the heat to a simmer and cover. Cook for 15–20 minutes, until done. Remove from the heat and fluff. Let stand for 5–10 minutes. Serve hot.

FRIED RICE
Chao Fan — Thailand

3–4 eggs, lightly beaten
salt, to taste
4 spring onions (scallions),
  sliced
1 tablespoon chopped ginger
3 tablespoons vegetable oil
125 g (¼ lb) cooked lamb,
  chicken, pork or ham, cut
  into ½ cm (¼ in.) cubes
50 g (2 oz) green peas,
  blanched
125 g (¼ lb) cooked prawns
  (shrimp), peeled
50 g (2 oz) carrot, julienned
1–2 tablespoons soy sauce
3 cups cold cooked rice

PROBABLY THE MOST FAMOUS and popular of rice dishes from Southeast Asia. Though Chinese in origin, it is cooked all over the East in some form or other. The ingredients change, but not the method. Here is a simple and fast version.

Method: Beat the eggs with a pinch of salt, half the spring onions and ½ tablespoon of the ginger. Heat 1 tablespoon of the oil in a hot wok. Add the eggs and stir-fry to a scramble. Remove the eggs from the wok and set aside.

Heat the rest of the oil and add the diced cooked meats, peas, prawns and carrot. Stir-fry for 1 minute. Stir in the soy sauce and remaining ginger. Add the rice. Stir-fry for 2–3 minutes while adding the remaining spring onions and eggs. Heat through and serve hot.

CHICKEN AND RICE
Murg Chawal — Sind

8–12 pieces chicken,
  (60 g, 2 oz each)
salt, to taste
1 tablespoon chopped ginger
1 tablespoon chopped garlic
3 tablespoons ghee or
  vegetable oil
2 bay leaves
2 green cardamom pods
2 cloves
1 large onion, chopped
1 tablespoon red chilli powder
¾ cup (185 g, 6 oz) rice
salt, to taste
¾ cup (185 mL, 6 fl oz) tomato
  purée
¾ cup (185 mL, 6 fl oz) water

THIS DISH FROM THE COSMOPOLITAN city of
Bombay has its origins in the Marathas, whose rice
dishes are famous along the west coast of India.
This is a non-vegetarian variation of a
vegetarian dish.

Method: Rub the chicken pieces with a little salt, half
the ginger, the garlic and 1 tablespoon of the ghee or
vegetable oil. Set aside.

Heat the remaining oil in a large saucepan. Add
the bay leaves, cardamom and cloves and allow to
sputter for a few seconds. Add the chicken pieces and
cook until sealed on all sides. Add the onion and stir-
fry for 2–3 minutes. Add the remaining ginger, chilli
powder and rice, stirring carefully to avoid breaking
the rice grains. Add the salt, the tomato purée and
the water.

Bring to a fast boil, then reduce the heat and
simmer with the lid on for 10–12 minutes, until the
rice is cooked. Remove from the heat, take off the lid
and fluff the rice with a roasting fork. Set aside for
5 minutes before serving.

CASHEW NUT AND PEA PULAO

Cashew Mattar Pulao — Deccan

3 tablespoons ghee or vegetable
  oil
½ tablespoon mustard seeds
⅓ tablespoon cumin seeds
2 tablespoons peanuts
3 tablespoons cashew nuts,
  chopped
100 g (3 oz) frozen or shelled
  green peas
a few curry leaves
½ tablespoon ground turmeric
1 cup (250 g, 8 oz) long-grain
  rice
2 cups (500 mL, 16 fl oz) water
salt, to taste
100 g (3 oz) grated (shredded)
  fresh or frozen coconut
2 tablespoons coriander
  (cilantro) leaves, chopped

A BLEND OF NORTH AND SOUTH Indian cuisines.
The tempering of rice with mustard seeds and
peanuts is very common in South Indian cuisine.
The tangy flavour of mustard seeds and the unique
flavour of curry leaves give this dish its character.

Method: Heat the ghee or vegetable oil in a saucepan.
Add the mustard seeds. When they start to splutter,
add the cumin seeds, peanuts, cashew nuts, peas,
curry leaves and turmeric. Stir-fry for 2-3 minutes.
Add the rice and fry carefully until the grains are
well coated in oil. Add the water and salt, stir well and
bring to a boil. Reduce the heat, cover and cook for
15–20 minutes, until done. Remove from the heat and
fluff with a roasting fork. Garnish with the grated
coconut and coriander and set aside for 5 minutes
before serving.

CURRIED NOODLES

Guay Teon Kaeng — Thailand

50 g (2 oz) broccoli florets
400 g (13 oz) rice vermicelli
2 tablespoons vegetable oil
375 g (³/₄ lb) beef, cut into
    strips
salt, to taste
3¹/₂ cups (850 mL, 28 fl oz)
    coconut milk
2 tablespoons curry powder
1 medium onion, sliced
2 tablespoons tamarind water
    (see glossary)
¹/₂ tablespoon sugar
2 tablespoons fish sauce
50 g (2 oz) bean sprouts
2 tablespoons raw peeled
    peanuts
a few coriander (cilantro)
    sprigs

ALTHOUGH RICE is the staple food of Thailand, noodles also put in an appearance on occasion, especially, as here, in combination dishes, which are quick and easy to prepare.

Method: Boil the broccoli in salted water and set aside. Cook the rice vermicelli as instructed on the packet and set aside. Heat the oil in a large saucepan. Add the beef, salt and 1¹/₂ cups (400 mL, 13 fl oz) of the coconut milk. Bring to a fast boil, reduce the heat and simmer for 8–10 minutes. When the beef is half-cooked and the liquid mostly evaporated, add the curry powder and onion. Stir-fry for about 5 minutes. Add the remaining coconut milk, tamarind water, sugar and fish sauce. Simmer for a further 3–5 minutes, until all the flavours have blended.

Arrange the vermicelli in serving bowls. Add the broccoli and bean sprouts. Spoon the beef and sauce on top and serve, garnished with a few peanuts and sprigs of coriander.

CLASSIC CHICKEN CURRY AND NOODLES

Panthe Kaukswe — Burma

CURRY

500 g (1 lb) chicken thigh
    fillets (tenderloin) cut into
    1 cm (½ in.) cubes
5 tablespoons vegetable oil
2 medium onions, chopped
2 tablespoons chopped ginger
1 tablespoon chopped garlic
2 tablespoons red chilli powder
1 tablespoon ground turmeric
salt, to taste
2½ cups (600 mL, 1 imp. pint)
    coconut milk
2 tablespoons chickpea flour
    (see glossary)
250 g (8 oz) thin egg noodles

ACCOMPANIMENTS

2 hard-boiled eggs, chopped
2 tablespoons coriander
    (cilantro) leaves, chopped
2 tablespoons chopped spring
    onions (scallions)
2 tablespoons crushed red
    chilli peppers
2 tablespoons crisp-fried egg
    noodles
4–6 lemon wedges

AN ALL-TIME FAVOURITE from Burma. I added this dish to the menu of a restaurant where I used to work ages ago, and am pleased to say that it still features there. I especially like the idea of the numerous accompaniments that are served with the dish, enhancing its presentation.

Method: Heat the oil in a large frying pan (skillet). Add the onion and cook until tender. Add the ginger, garlic, chilli powder, turmeric and chicken. Add the salt and stir-fry for 2–3 minutes. Pour in the coconut milk, bring to a fast boil, then reduce the heat and simmer for 8–10 minutes, until nearly done.

Place the chickpea flour in a bowl. Add a little water and whisk to a smooth paste. Add this to the curry and cook for a further 5 minutes.

Meanwhile, cook the noodles and keep them warm. Place the noodles in a dish and serve topped with the curry. Serve the accompaniments separately, for each diner to add according to individual taste.

SPICY NOODLES

Mee Goreng — Singapore

400 g (13 oz) yellow egg noodles
4 tablespoons sesame oil
2 eggs
salt, to taste
100 g (3 oz) bean curd, cut into
   1 cm (½ in.) cubes
2 medium onions, sliced
2 tablespoons chopped ginger
1 medium potato, boiled and
   diced
1 tablespoon soy sauce
3 tablespoons tomato sauce
   (ketchup)
2 tablespoons chilli sauce
3 sliced green chilli peppers
4 spring onions (scallions),
   sliced
1 tablespoon coriander
   (cilantro) leaves, chopped

THIS TYPICAL SINGAPOREAN dish combines elements of Indian and Chinese cuisines. Its origins seem to have been very similar to those of American Chop Suey — a handful of ingredients thrown in together.

Method: Boil the noodles. Drain, rinse under cold water, add a little sesame oil and set aside.

Whisk the eggs with a pinch of salt. Make a flat omelette and lay out to cool. Roll and cut into roundels.

Meanwhile, heat the remaining oil in a wok and fry the bean curd. When brown, remove from the wok and set aside. Add the onion to the wok and stir-fry for 1–2 minutes. Add the ginger and noodles and toss for 3–4 minutes. Add the potatoes, soy sauce, bean curd, tomato sauce, chilli sauce and chilli peppers. Toss for a few minutes.

Just before serving, add the spring onions and the omelette roundels. Serve on a plate, garnished with the coriander.

EGG NOODLES WITH CURRY SAUCE
Kao Sai — Thailand

CURRY
50 g (2 oz) coconut cream
2 tablespoons red curry paste
375 g (¾ lb) chicken, cut into
small pieces
1 tablespoon fish sauce
2 tablespoons soy sauce
2 cups (500 mL, 16 fl oz)
coconut milk
juice of 1 lime
3 tablespoons vegetable oil
300 g (10 oz) egg noodles,
cooked

ACCOMPANIMENTS
60 g (2 oz) fried egg noodles
2 spring onions (scallions),
sliced
2 red chilli peppers, sliced

A VERY POPULAR DISH of Burmese origin, very similar to Kaukswe, but again with a special Thai stamp. It is usually sold in the food stalls of Chiang Mai, and can be cooked using any meats. The noodles are served in a bowl, with the curry on top of them. The accompaniments are served separately, for each diner to add according to individual taste.

Method: Heat the coconut cream in a large pan, and allow to cook until the oil starts to separate. Stir occasionally. Add the red curry paste and stir-fry for 1–2 minutes. Add the chicken and stir-fry for a further 1–2 minutes. Add the fish sauce, soy sauce and coconut milk. Cook over a medium heat for 8–10 minutes, until done. Finish off by adding the lime juice. Check the seasoning and add salt if necessary.

While the chicken is cooking, heat the oil and add the chilli peppers. Fry over a low heat until they turn a dark brownish red. Remove and set aside. Serve as an accompaniment.

Place the noodles in a bowl and spoon some curry on top. Serve the garnishes separately.

LAKSA

Singapore

250 g (½ lb) chicken, cut into strips
4 cups (1 L, 1¾ imp. pints) water
salt, to taste
2 tablespoons sesame oil
3 spring onions (scallions), sliced
1 tablespoon chopped ginger
1 tablespoon chopped garlic
½ tablespoon ground turmeric
1 tablespoon ground coriander
150 g (5 oz) rice noodles
125 g (¼ lb) peeled prawns (shrimp)
100 g (3 oz) bean curd, cut into strips
½ tablespoon black peppecorns, crushed
¾ cup (185 mL, 6 fl oz) coconut milk
50 g (2 oz) bean sprouts
2 tablespoons coriander (cilantro) leaves, chopped

PROBABLY THE MOST FAMOUS of Southeast Asian dishes, this is not just a soup, but a meal in itself. A combination of rice noodles, meat and seafood, it forms a perfect meal. A spicy sambal usually accompanies the laksa — to spice it up if you want to.

Method: Place the chicken in the water, add the salt and bring to a fast boil. Reduce the heat and simmer for 10–15 minutes, until the chicken is nearly done. Remove and strain, keeping the stock and chicken separate.

Heat the oil in a wok or deep pan. Add the spring onions, ginger and garlic, and stir-fry for 2–3 minutes. Add the turmeric and coriander. Stir for 1 minute, then add the chicken stock. Bring to a fast boil, then reduce the heat and simmer for about 10 minutes.

Meanwhile, boil the rice noodles. Strain then wash them in cold water, and toss with a little oil to stop the noodles sticking together.

Add the chicken, prawns, bean curd, peppercorns, coconut milk and noodles. Simmer for 2–3 minutes. Add the bean sprouts and coriander leaves. Check the seasoning and adjust with salt if necessary. Serve hot.

CURRY PASTES & POWDERS

THE ART OF MAKING a good curry lies in the blending of the spices — freshly ground ones if possible. The curry powder sold in cans is fairly dull and can overpower other flavours. Try to grind your spices fresh, and store any leftover powder in an airtight container in a cool place.

Though grinding spices is still a daily chore for many women in rural areas of Asia, powders are popular in cities. There, people usually buy spices from the same shop for years because of quality and consistency. Some spices, such as red chillies, turmeric, salt and asafoetida, are almost always bought as a powder. However, once you start cooking with freshly ground spices it is very difficult to return to ready-made powders.

A word of caution when drying whole spices: dry them over very low heat so as not to alter their flavour. I find they dry well in a cooling oven recently switched off after cooking some other food.

When making curry paste, be sure to oven- or pan-dry hard spices before powdering them in a spice or coffee grinder. If powdering sweet spices, such as cinnamon, cardamom or nutmeg, be sure your grinder is absolutely dry and free of other spice residue.

GREEN CURRY PASTE

Krung Kaeng Khieu Wan — Thailand

1 tablespoon coriander seeds
1 tablespoon cumin seeds
5 whole black peppercorns
2 large handfuls coarsely
    chopped coriander (cilantro)
    roots, stems and leaves
a few Kaffir lime leaves
1 tablespoon chopped garlic
2 tablespoons sliced spring
    onions (scallions)
6–8 green chilli peppers, stems
    discarded, chopped
1 tablespoon galangal
1 teaspoon (Thai) shrimp paste
3 stalks lemon grass
2 teaspoons fish sauce
2 tablespoons vegetable oil
2 tablespoons Kaffir lime peel

Makes enough for a 4-person dish.

ONE OF THE MOST popular curries from Thailand is the green curry. As in the cuisine of South India, wet pastes form the basis of Thai curries. In most cases, coconut milk is added to the paste to make the curry; water is often added, too.

Method: Dry-roast the coriander and cumin and peppercorns in a heavy saucepan until fragrant. Grind to a powder in a spice or coffee grinder. Transfer to a blender or food processor. Add the coriander roots, stems and leaves, Kaffir lime leaves, garlic, spring onions, chilli peppers, galangal, shrimp paste, lemon grass, fish sauce, vegetable oil and lime peel. Blend or process into a smooth paste, adding a little water if necessary.

    This paste will last for a few weeks if refrigerated. Simply spoon into a jar and cover with a film of vegetable oil. Seal tightly and refrigerate until needed.

RED CURRY PASTE

Kaeng Phed — Thailand

6–7 dried red chilli peppers
2 teaspoons black peppercorns
2 teaspoons cumin seeds
4 small red onions, chopped
2 stalks lemon grass
3 cloves garlic
1 tablespoon chopped galangal
2 tablespoons chopped
coriander (cilantro) stems,
leaves and roots
1 cm (½ in.) piece of blachan,
dry-roasted (see glossary)
2 tablespoons vegetable oil
1 tablespoon fish sauce

Make enough for a 4-person dish.

THIS PASTE IS USED mostly with any meat, fish or vegetables. Like its green cousin, it is one of the basics of Thai cuisine.

Method: Dry-roast the chilli peppers, peppercorns and cumin seeds in a heavy saucepan until fragrant. Grind to a powder in a spice or coffee grinder. Transfer to a blender or food processor. Add the onion, lemon grass, garlic, galangal, coriander stems, leaves and roots, blachan, vegetable oil and fish sauce. Blend or process into a smooth paste, adding a little water if necessary.

This paste will last for several weeks if refrigerated in a screw-top jar. Simply spoon into the jar and cover with a film of vegetable oil. Seal tightly and refrigerate until needed.

MUSLIM CURRY PASTE

Krung Kaeng Masaman — Thailand

6–8 red chilli peppers
a little hot water
1 tablespoon cumin seeds
1 tablespoon coriander seeds
2 teaspoons black peppercorns
½ star anise
4 green (small) cardamom
*   pods*
3 stalks lemon grass, sliced
6 whole cloves
2 teaspoons mace
5 cm (2 in.) piece of cinnamon
*   stick*
1 tablespoon galangal, chopped
2 medium spring onions
(scallions), chopped
5 cloves garlic
1 tablespoon (Thai) shrimp
*   paste*
2 tablespoons vegetable oil

Makes enough for 4-person dish.

ALTHOUGH THE ORIGIN of this paste is Indian, the Thais have introduced their own touch by adding lemon grass and shrimp paste. It can be used with most meats and vegetables.

Method: Coarsely chop the chilli peppers. Place in a bowl and cover with hot water. Set aside to soak for 10–15 minutes.

Combine the cumin seeds, coriander seeds, black peppercorns, star anise, cardamom, lemon grass, cloves, mace and cinnamon in a large, heavy saucepan. Dry-roast over a medium heat for 5–7 minutes, taking care not to scorch any ingredients. (Alternatively, place in a roasting pan and roast in a preheated oven at 120°C (250°F / gas mark ½) for 20–30 minutes.) Allow to cool then grind to a powder in a spice or coffee grinder.

Place in a blender or food processor. Add the galangal, spring onions, garlic, shrimp paste and vegetable oil. Drain the chilli peppers, reserving the water to make the paste. Add the chilli peppers to the blender or processor. Blend or process into a paste, adding a little of the reserved water to make the paste smooth.

This paste will last for several weeks if refrigerated in a screw-top jar. Simply spoon into the jar and cover with a film of vegetable oil. Seal tightly and refrigerate until needed.

CEYLON CURRY POWDER

Ceylon

6 tablespoons coriander seeds
4 tablespoons cumin seeds
6–8 whole black peppercorns
6–8 whole dried red chilli
   peppers
2 teaspoons mustard seeds
2 teaspoons fenugreek seeds
6–8 dried curry leaves
2–3 bay leaves
2 tablespoons ground turmeric

Makes 15 tablespoons.

ALTHOUGH INDIAN AND CEYLONESE (Sri Lankan) curry powders have very similar ingredients, their flavours are subtly different. In the Indian curry powders, the spices are not roasted, but slightly toasted in a warm oven to facilitate blending. In Sri Lankan curry powders, the raw spices are dry-roasted to give a fragrant, spicy flavour. If you make your own curry powder, prepare only small quantities at a time and store in an airtight container to ensure maximum freshness and flavour.

Method: Heat a wok over a low heat. Add the coriander and cumin seeds, black peppercorns, chilli peppers, mustard and fenugreek seeds, curry leaves and bay leaves. Dry-roast the spices until fragrant. Allow to cool. Grind to a fine powder in a spice or coffee grinder. Mix in the ground turmeric and store in an airtight container. The powder will keep for 2–3 weeks.

GARAM MASALA

India

1 tablespoon cardamom seeds
4 cm (1½ in.) piece of
     cinnamon stick
1 teaspoon whole black
     peppercorns
1 teaspoon cloves
1 teaspoon cumin seeds
1 teaspoon fennel seeds
Makes 2½ tablespoons.

THIS SPICE MIXTURE is often used to finish Indian dishes. Everyone has their own recipe — here is one I find excellent.

Method: Dry-roast all the ingredients in a heavy saucepan. Allow to cool. Grind to a powder in a spice or coffee grinder. Store in an airtight container for 4–5 weeks.

KASHMIRI MASALA

Kashmir

2 tablespoons fennel seeds
1 tablespoon cardamom seeds
6 bay leaves
2 tablespoons mace
Makes 6 tablespoons.

THIS MASALA IS USED in a large number of vegetarian dishes. I find the flavour subtle and not as overpowering as *garam masala*. It should be made in small quantities only so that it retains its freshness.

Method: Mix all the ingredients in a small bowl. Grind to a powder in a spice or coffee grinder. Store in an airtight container.

GLOSSARY

Most of the ingredients listed below are available from Asian food stores. Alternatives are suggested for more difficult-to-find items. Many commonly used ingredients are also stocked in Western-style supermarkets.

ALLSPICE

Berry of the pimento tree. Usually purchased as a powder.

AMCHUR

(see Mango)

ASAFOETIDA

A resinous flavouring with a garlic-like smell, used in minute quantities. Available in the form of a reddish-brown powder or crystals from Indian food stores.

BAMBOO SHOOTS

Available in cans in larger supermarkets or Asian food stores, they impart a delicate flavour to soups and sambals.

BANANA LEAVES

Used for decoration and to seal in juices, these may be found in Asian markets. Wash before use and immerse in hot water to soften before folding. If unavailable, use foil for the cooking process, then arrange the finished food on an attractive serving dish.

BASIL

There are many varieties of basil; those specified in this book are: **Holy basil**, a sweet-tasting, purplish leaf normally added towards the end of cooking; **Thai basil**, a shiny green leaf with a licorice-like taste. Also added towards the end of cooking.

BLACHAN

A dark-brown flavouring made of dried shrimp paste, and available in cans or slabs. The smell is very pungent, but decreases during cooking. Blachan keeps indefinitely if stored in a tightly sealed jar.

CANDLE NUT

An oily nut used for its flavour and to thicken curries. If unavailable, substitute pine nuts, cashew nuts or almonds.

CARDAMOM

Black or green pods containing fragrant seeds. Used mainly in meat dishes or sprinkled on in powder form at the end of cooking.

CASHEW NUT

A sweet, kidney-shaped nut sold raw in Asian stores.

CHILLIES

Chillies are small capsicums used to add heat to any dish. They range in colour from green through yellow to red. Generally speaking, the smaller the chilli, the hotter its taste. **Chilli powder** is made from ground red chillies and is hotter than the Mexican variety. **Green chillies** are sometimes ground (seeds removed) for use in sambals. **Jalapeño chillies** are used especially in Thai recipes; they are dark green and extremely hot. They can replace Serrano chillies. **Kashmiri chillies** are mild, red peppers, less pungent than red chillies. **Red chillies** are used whole or chopped for hot flavouring, or sliced as a garnish. **Serrano chillies** are very dark green and very hot. They can replace jalapeño chillies.

CILANTRO

(see Coriander)

CINNAMON

A fragrant bark available in supermarkets in stick or powder form.

CLOVES

The dried buds of a tropical tree, cloves are sold whole or powdered.

COCONUT CREAM

A liquid extracted from the first pressing and straining of grated coconut flesh and water. As the name suggests, coconut cream is thicker and richer than coconut milk. Available in cans or as a block.

COCONUT MILK

A liquid extracted from the second pressing and straining of grated coconut flesh or desiccated coconut. Readily available in cans. Do not buy the sweetened variety used for tropical drinks.

CORIANDER

A pungent herb, used in the form of whole seeds, powdered seeds or fresh. The leafy part of the plant is also known as cilantro.

CUMIN

White or black seeds with a nutty flavour and strong scent. Used whole or ground, cumin is one of the basics of Indian cuisine.

CURRY LEAVES

Available fresh or dried, these leaves of an Asian tree are usually the first ingredient fried during curry preparation to impart a piquant flavour to the oil.

DHAL

General term for a dish made with lentils or other pulses. The most frequently used are: yellow lentils (*toovar dhal*), pink lentils (*masar dhal*), mung beans (*moon dhal*), black gram beans (*urad dhal*), yellow split peas (*channa dhal*).

FENNEL SEEDS

Greenish-brown seeds of common fennel, available whole or ground.

FENUGREEK

Small, brown, bittersweet seeds available whole or ground. The taste is slightly like aniseed.

FISH SAUCE

The liquid extract from salted, fermented anchovies. Use strictly according to the recipe to avoid over-salting the dish.

GALANGAL

A rhizome of the ginger family, available fresh, frozen, dried and powdered. For preference, use fresh if available or dried (reduce quantity by one third).

GARAM MASALA

A powdered mixture of coriander, cumin, black peppercorns, cardamom, cinnamon, cloves and nutmeg.

GHEE

Clarified butter, used to impart a distinctive taste to curries. Ghee can be heated to higher temperatures than butter, without burning.

GINGER

Fresh root ginger is used peeled and chopped in most of the recipes in this book.

KAFFIR LIME LEAVES

Used extensively in Thai cuisine, and often available fresh in Asian stores. Do not use dried or frozen leaves, as these do not have the fragrance of the fresh leaf. If unavailable, substitute lime leaves or zest.

KARAI

A deep, curved-sided cooking vessel from India. A wok may be substituted.

KIM CHI

Korean pickled cabbage, sold in jars or cans in Asian food stores.

LAOS POWDER

The dried root of galangal; very delicate in flavour.

LEMON GRASS

An aromatic grass, its whitish stem is used to impart a lemon flavour to curries.

MACE

The membrane around the fruit of the nutmeg tree. It is commonly available in powder form.

MANGO, DRIED GREEN (AMCHUR)

Usually available as a powder.

MUSTARD SEEDS

Small, black seeds used whole or ground in savoury dishes.

OIL

Peanut oil is high in mono-unsaturates and is used widely in Southeast Asian cuisines. Most recipes in this book specify **vegetable oil** for its mild flavour, high smoke point and long shelf life. Vegetable oils are low in polyunsaturates.

PALM SUGAR

A sugar obtained from the sap of coconut and Palmyra palms by boiling until it crystalises. Usually sold in large lumps in Asian food stores. Also known as *jaggery.*

PANCH PHORAN

A mixture of 5 whole spices: 1 tablespoon mustard seeds, 1 tablespoon cumin seeds, 1 tablespoon nigella seeds (*kalonji*), ¼ tablespoon fenugreek seeds, ½ tablespoon fennel seeds.

PEPPERCORNS

Tropical berries, black after sun-drying of the whole berry, and white after soaking to remove the outer covering (pericarp).

RICE

Basmati rice is a scented Indian rice used mainly on special occasions. **Jasmine rice** is a scented rice used for everyday cooking in India, and readily available in the West.

RICE NOODLES

Very fine noodles requiring only brief preparation by soaking in hot water. They can be crisp-fried instead of soaking.

SAFFRON

The most expensive spice in the world, saffron is obtained by drying the stamens of the saffron crocus. Dark orange in colour and with a strong aroma, saffron is used extensively in northern Indian cuisine.

SAMBAL ULEK

A paste made of chillies and salt, which can be used in cooking or as an accompaniment. Also spelled Sambal oelek.

SESAME OIL

Oil obtained from roasted sesame seeds, used only as a flavouring, not for frying.

SHRIMP PASTE

(see Blachan)

SOY SAUCE

An essential ingredient of Asian cuisine, soy sauce imparts a salty flavour. Light soy is preferred for soup or seafood dishes, where the colour of the dish is to be retained. Indonesian soy (*kecap manis*) is thicker and sweeter than the Chinese or Japanese varieties. All varieties keep indefinitely without refrigeration.

SPRING (OR GREEN) ONIONS (SCALLIONS)

The white stem and green leaf of two onion varieties that do not form a bulb.

TAMARIND WATER

Make by breaking off 3 tablespoons of tamarind block and soaking in 1½ cups hot water for 4–5 minutes. Break up the tamarind with a fork or the back of a spoon to make a watery paste, then strain and use as directed.

THAI EGGPLANTS

Pea-sized berries that grow in clusters. Their bitter taste contrasts with the richness of the curry. If unavailable, substitute green peas to achieve the same appearance, if not the same taste.

TURMERIC

An orange-yellow powder made from a rhizome of the ginger family. Used for its distinctive taste and colour, turmeric should not be used in place of saffron, or vice versa.

INDEX

Baby calamari with bamboo shoots, 38
Banana chilli curry, 103
Battered prawns in curry sauce, 30
Beef
 beef *baffat,* 95
 beef hot pot, 96
 beef *rendang,* 97
 beef with apricots, 94
 beef with potatoes in Muslim curry, 93
 coconut beef curry, 92
 *kadai-*cooked beef, 98
 sour beef stew, 99
Beef *Baffat,* 95
Beef hot pot, 96
Beef *rendang,* 97
Beef with apricots, 94
Beef with potatoes in Muslim curry, 93

Calamari
 baby, with bamboo shoots, 38
 in red curry, 39
Caramelised chicken with ginger and coriander (cilantro), 49
Cashew nut and pea *pulao,* 121
Cauliflower with fennel and ginger, 106
Ceylon curry paste, 133
Ceylon prawn curry, 29
Chettinad lamb and coconut, 74
Chicken
 caramelised chicken with ginger and coriander (cilantro), 49
 chicken and rice, 120
 chicken and yoghurt with cardamom and ginger, 47
 chicken *cafreal,* 58
 chicken *coorgi,* 61
 chicken pistachio, 48
 chicken with cardamom, 60
 chicken with chilli vinegar and pickled cabbage, 46

chicken with potato and onion, 57
chicken with yoghurt, 45
curry
 chicken and potato curry, 54
 chicken curry with lemon grass, 59
 chicken curry with soy sauce, 52
 chicken curry with tamarind, 51
 dry chicken curry, 56
 green chicken curry with eggplant, 44
 lampries curry, 50
 sliced chicken with holy basil, 55
 spicy chicken wings, 53
Chicken and potato curry, 54
Chicken and rice, 120
Chicken and yoghurt with cardamom and ginger, 47
Chicken *cafreal,* 58
Chicken *coorgi,* 61
Chicken curry with lemon grass, 59
Chicken curry with soy sauce, 52
Chicken curry with tamarind, 51
Chicken pistachio, 48
Chicken with cardamom, 60
Chicken with lemon grass, 59
Chicken with potato and onion, 57
Chicken with yoghurt, 45
Chickpeas with ginger, 107
Classic chicken curry and noodles, 123
Coconut and sesame rice, 116
Coconut beef curry, 92
Coconut rice, 115
Crab
 in the shell, 37
 Spice Coast, 36
Cumin rice, 114
Curried noodles, 122
Curry Pastes & Powders
 Ceylon curry, 133

garam masala, 134
green curry, 130
Kashmiri *masala,* 134
Muslim curry, 132
red curry, 131

Dry chicken curry, 56
Duck
 spicy, curry, 62
 Penang, curry, 63
 Rangoon roast, 64
 with green chilli, 65

Egg noodles with curry sauce, 125
Eggplant with lentils and spices, 108
Everyday prawn curry, 32

Fish
 caldine, 19
 grilled snapper with green mango chutney, 16
 marinated, in curry sauce, 18
 marinated, with mustard, 26
 Parsee, with mint chutney, 24
 shallow-fried, Mekong, 17
 sweet and sour, 25
 whole snapper with peppers, 20
 whole, in red sauce, 27
 with fenugreek leaves, 21
 with soy sauce, pan-fried, 23
 with tomatoes and tamarind, 22
Fish *caldine,* 19
Fish with fenugreek leaves, 21
Fish with soy sauce, pan-fried, 23
Fish with tomatoes and tamarind, 22
Fried rice, 119

garam masala, 134
Green chicken curry with eggplant, 44
Green curry, 130

Grilled snapper with green
    mango chutney, 16

Kadai-cooked beef, 98
Kashmiri masala, 134
Katha lamb curry, 70

Laksa, 126
Lamb
    Chettinad, and coconut, 74
    in yoghurt with spices, 79
    Katha, curry, 70
    korma, 69
    Mogul, with dried nuts, 77
    Sindhi, 73
    spicy, 76
    with almonds, 78
    with chilli, 68
    with figs, 75
    with potatoes, 71
    with yoghurt, 72
Lamb in yoghurt with
    spices, 79
Lamb korma, 69
Lamb with almonds, 78
Lamb with chilli, 68
Lamb with figs, 75
Lamb with potatoes, 71
Lamb with yoghurt, 72
Lampries curry, 50
Lemon rice, 117

Marinated fish in curry
    sauce, 18
Marinated fish with
    mustard, 26
Marinated fried prawns, 33
Mixed vegetable curry, 102
Mogul lamb with dried nuts, 77
Mushrooms with dried fruits
    and poppy seeds, 105
Muslim curry, 132

Noodles
    classic chicken curry
        and, 123
    curried, 122
    egg, with curry sauce, 125
    laksa, 126
    spicy, 124

Omelette soup with pork and
    coriander (cilantro), 10

Pan-fried pork cutlets, 87
Penang duck curry, 63
Pineapple shrimp curry, 34
Pork
    curry, 82
    with ginger, 84
    cutlets with green
        peppercorns, 85
    in coconut milk, 83
    kebabs, 86
    pan-fried, cutlets, 87
    spare ribs with soy and
        ginger, 88
Pork curry, 82
Pork curry with ginger, 84
Pork cutlets with green
    peppercorns, 85
Pork in coconut milk, 83
Pork kebabs, 86
Prawns see also Shrimp
    battered, in curry sauce, 30
    Ceylon, curry, 29
    curry with Thai
        eggplant, 28
    everyday, curry, 32
    marinated fried, 33
    spicy, in coconut milk, 31
Prawn curry with Thai
    eggplant, 28

Rangoon roast duck, 64
Red curry, 131
Rice
    cashew nut and pea
        pulao, 121
    chicken and, 120
    coconut, 115
    coconut and sesame, 116
    cumin, 114
    fried, 119
    lemon, 117
    yellow, 118
Rice soup with prawns
    (shrimp), 11

Scallops
    in roasted chilli sauce, 40
Seafood and lemon grass
    soup, 13
Shallow-fried fish Mekong, 17
Shrimp see also Prawns
    in coconut and fennel, 35
    pineapple, curry, 34

Shrimp in coconut and
    fennel, 35
Sindhi lamb, 73
Sliced chicken with holy
    basil, 55
Soups
    omelette, with pork and
        coriander (cilantro), 10
    rice, with prawns
        (shrimp), 11
    seafood and lemon grass, 13
    spicy chicken, with prawns
        (shrimp), 12
Sour beef stew, 99
Spare ribs with soy and
    ginger, 88
Spice Coast crab, 36
Spiced chickpeas with
    tomatoes and coriander, 104
Spiced small potatoes, 109
Spicy chicken soup with
    prawns (shrimp), 12
Spicy chicken wings, 53
Spicy duck curry, 62
Spicy lamb, 76
Spicy noodles, 124
Spicy prawns in coconut
    milk, 31
Squid see Calamari
Sweet and sour fish, 25

Vegetable rolls, 110
Vegetables & Legumes
    banana chilli curry, 103
    cauliflower with fennel and
        ginger, 106
    chickpeas with ginger, 107
    eggplant with lentils and
        spices, 108
    mixed vegetable curry, 102
    mushrooms with dried
        fruits and poppy
        seeds, 105
    spiced chickpeas with
        tomatoes and
        coriander, 104
    spiced small potatoes, 109
    vegetable rolls, 110

Whole fish in red sauce, 27
Whole snapper with
    peppers, 20

Yellow rice, 118

ACKNOWLEDGEMENTS

I WOULD LIKE to take this opportunity to acknowledge the invaluable assistance of my wife Sita without whose research and testing of various recipes this book would not be possible. I would also like to thank my literary agent Ms Jane Adams, Ms Susan Morris-Yates, Publisher, and Mr Angus Cameron for editing the manuscript. I am grateful to my staff at Bombay Heritage, especially my colleague Mr Kermani for his continuous support. Last but not least, I would like to thank my family, especially my brother Sanjoy for always being ready to taste and comment on the various dishes.